hand crafted

BEAUTIFUL THINGS TO CREATE AT HOME

HOUSE & GARDEN

hand crafted

BEAUTIFUL THINGS TO CREATE AT HOME

acp
books

contents

fabric & yarn — 8

paper — 62

cooking — 94

gift baskets

116

garden

130

home

156

welcome to *hand crafted*

There's nothing I love more than starting a new craft project. For me, there's immense satisfaction to be had in CREATING SOMETHING WITH MY OWN TWO HANDS, and in watching all that careful effort evolve into a treasured item. That's the BEAUTY OF CRAFT – it's a way of personalising your world and expressing your own creativity, even if it's just a small undertaking, like embellishing table linen. This book is a fantastic introduction to the world of craft and the pleasures it can bring. Inside, you'll find all manner of inspiring projects that range from THE PLEASINGLY SIMPLE, LIKE STENCILLING A MIRROR, to more complex projects such as knitting, or making silhouettes. One thing you'll notice as soon as you start flipping through this book is how wonderfully modern and downright gorgeous each and every project is. You'll want to do them all! I hope this will inspire a whole new generation to join in the fun of craft and to find out JUST HOW REWARDING IT CAN BE. Enjoy!

Maya

Maya Kelett, *Australian House & Garden*

fabric & yarn

equipment

In an age of easy consumerism, we begin to crave the charm of the handmade item. MASS PRODUCTION HAS BROUGHT WITH IT A CERTAIN BOREDOM. Where are those gentle imperfections that mark out an object as being individual? Where is the personality? The projects in this chapter bring back that appeal to everyday items, TRANSFORMING THE STORE-BOUGHT INTO SOMETHING SPECIAL. A little skill is required, but PATIENCE IS MORE IMPORTANT THAN EXPERIENCE. The embroidery is unfussy, the beading and appliqué is easy. Many of the ideas adapt ready-made pieces, while other items are made from scratch. THE EMPHASIS IS ON SIMPLICITY, so don't be afraid to thread a needle, lay out a piece of fabric or unfurl some yarn. There's a lot of joy to be had in creating something yourself.

PINS & NEEDLES
Steel dressmaking pins at least 2.5cm long are the best choice for sewing. Glass-headed pins, which are made from needle rejects, are sharp but their heads can break. Needles come in different varieties, so use the right one for the job. A sharps needle is of medium length, with a small eye, and is used with sewing cotton or one strand of stranded embroidery cotton. An embroidery (or crewel) needle is long and sharp, with a large eye. Use it with stranded embroidery thread and Perle cotton. A tapestry needle has a blunt tip and is not suitable for embroidery. A beading needle has a fine, long shaft and a small narrow eye so it may be easily threaded through beads.

SEWING MACHINE
Sewing machines range from basic models that do straight and zigzag stitching, to computerised machines that can sew buttonholes by measuring the button for you. Whatever machine you have, take the time to read the manual and find out about its features. And have it serviced regularly; like your car, a sewing machine has an engine that should be looked after. Most home sewing can be done using straight stitch and zigzag, although having a four-step buttonhole function does make that particular job a lot easier. Use medium-length stitches for general sewing, shorter stitches for finer fabrics and longer stitches for heavier fabrics.

SCISSORS

For cutting fabric you need a pair of good quality dressmaker's shears (with blades 20cm/8 inches long) or more heavy-duty tailor's shears (with 25cm/ 10-inch blades). They have a bent-handle design that makes it easier to cut on a flat surface, and there are scissors specially made for left-handers. Never use the shears for cutting paper as it ruins the blades. Tie a ribbon around the handle to identify them as being for fabric only.

A smaller pair of sharp scissors may be used for snipping threads, and pinking shears, which make a zigzag cut, are useful for neatening seams to reduce fraying.

TAPE MEASURE

Accurate measuring is a building block for success in sewing. To get it right, you'll need a tape measure marked in centimetres and millimetres (some also have inch measurements). The best choice is a fibreglass tape as it won't stretch out of shape. Remember, too, that a dressmaker's measuring tape is 1.5cm wide, the standard width for a seam allowance; this makes pinning seams much easier. You'll also find that pressing fabric and seams with an iron as you go helps with accuracy.

NEEDLES & HOOKS

A knitting needle or crochet hook's size is based on its diameter; the size is indicated in millimetres. The higher the number, the thicker the needle or hook. These tools may be made of metal, plastic, wood or bamboo. All work well, but some people have a preference for using bamboo or wood as the needles are warmer to hold and stitches don't slip off as easily as on metal or plastic. Although it's better to use the needle or hook size indicated in a pattern, what is more important is that you're getting the correct tension. In knitting, this means that you have the same number of stitches and rows over a 10cm square that the pattern specifies. If you find you're making too few stitches, change to a finer needle; if there are too many, use a thicker needle to compensate.

YARN

Yarn describes any spun thread. In knitting and crochet, yarn may be wool, cotton, a man-made fibre, or a blend of these. Unfortunately there isn't a simple connection between the term ply and a yarn's thickness. A single thread may be spun thick or thin, and ply simply refers to the number of single threads twisted together to make the yarn. If you want to use a wool other than what's specified in a pattern, knit a 10cm square to check that you'll get the correct tension. It's also important to buy yarn from the same dye lot, as there will be small variations in colour between the different lots. The easiest way to do this is to buy enough yarn for the pattern in one go.

CARBON AND MARKERS

Dressmaker's carbon is the tried and true way to transfer embroidery designs. Place the carbon paper on top of the fabric, and a photocopy of the design on top of the carbon, then use a sharp pencil to trace over the design. The carbon marks will come off in the wash. Dressmaker's carbon may also be used with a tracing wheel to mark lines for sewing.

Disappearing, or fade-out, marking pens are very handy for marking lines for sewing. Some use ink that fades away in 48 to 72 hours, while others have ink that is erased with water.

embellished nightdress

The simple addition of an appliqué flower and touches of embroidery transform a cotton slip into an appealing summer nightdress.

Materials

cotton petticoat

appliqué flower, either bought from a craft/haberdashery store or unpicked from a doily

2 skeins DMC stranded embroidery cotton, one in aqua and one in bright green. We used Bright Chartreuse (704) and Light Turquoise (598). Use six strands for all stitching in this project.

embroidery needle

Method

1. Pin, then tack appliqué flower in place on nightdress.

2. Using the aqua thread, work a line of backstitch in the centre of each petal, as shown. Secure end of thread firmly with a knot on the wrong side. In the centre of the flower, work a circle of running stitch in the aqua thread. In the same circle, work a round of running stitch in the bright green thread, working the green stitches in the spaces between the aqua ones to create an unbroken line of stitches for the circle. Sew a few stitches of both colours in the flower's centre.

3. Using aqua thread, work a line of running stitch along both straps. Catch the top of the flower in the stitching to hold it in place.

4. Work a line of running stitch around the neckline. Use the bright green thread to work another line of running stitch that matches the first, as in the photo.

5. Remove tacking stitches from flower.

STITCHING THE FLOWER
The embroidery on the flower is also practical, as it actually holds it in place. Make sure you stitch right through the flower so it's well secured.

WORKING THE BORDER
The running stitch around the neckline and on the straps is easy to do. For the best result, try to keep the second row of stitches exactly matching the first row.

TIP
The key to making running stitch look great is to keep the stitches even. On fabrics with a slightly coarser weave, you can count the number of threads that each stitch covers. After a while, you'll find you can keep the stitches the same length without much effort.

snuggly bed socks

Keep your toes warm on a winter's evening with these subtly striped socks, or pull them on first thing in the morning when the frost is still on the ground.

Materials

main colour (M): 2 balls (50g each) 8ply wool
   (we used Cleckheaton Tapestry 19
   – camel, undyed, soft blue and dusty lilac)
contrast (C): 1 ball (50g) 8ply wool (we
   used Cleckheaton Crepe in colour 2251
   – dusty aqua)
1 pair 4mm (No.8) knitting needles
1 spare 4mm (No.8) knitting needle
2 stitch holders

(TENSION: 22STS AND 30 ROWS OVER 10CM)

KEY
K = knit stitch
P = purl stitch
K2tog = knit two together

Method

Using M, cast on 48 stitches
1st row: K2 * P1 K1 repeat from * to end of row.
Repeat this row 33 times or until you have the desired length.
With right side facing, proceed as follows to make the top of the foot:
1st row: Using M, K32, turn, leave remaining stitches on stitch holder.
2nd row: Using M, K16, turn, leave remaining 16 stitches on holder.
Join in C and work garter stitch 52 rows on these 16 stitches.
Break off yarn.

Using M and the 16 stitches left on the stitch holder, knit to the end of the row.
Next row: Using M, K16 then knit up 27sts from side of instep, then K8 along toe. Leave these stitches on one needle. Using the spare needle, knit remaining 8 toe stitches; knit up 27sts from other side of instep and remaining 16sts (102sts).

Work following rows in garter stitch for the stripes in the foot. The stitches are held on two needles, and you use the spare needle to do the actual knitting.
Rows 1 to 3: Using M, knit to end of row.
Rows 4 to 7: Using C, knit to end of row.
Rows 8 to 11: Using M, knit to end of row.
Rows 12 to 15: Using C, knit to end of row.
Row 16: Using M, knit to end of row.
Row 17: Using M, (start decreasing) K1 K2tog. K46 (K2tog) twice, K46 K2tog. K1 (98 sts)
Row 18: Using M, K1 K2tog. K44 (K2tog) twice, K44 K2tog. K1 (94 sts)
Row 19: Using M, K1 K2 tog. K42 (K2tog) twice, K42 K2tog. K1 (90 sts)
Row 20: Using C, K1 K2tog. K40 (K2tog) twice, K40 K2tog. K1 (86 sts).
Row 21 to 23: Using C, K to end of row on these 86 sts.
Row 24: Cast off using C.
Use a flat seam to make up.

NOTE Garter stitch means to knit every row.
This makes a sock 23cm long to fit women's feet.

THE TOP OF THE FOOT
After you have completed the ankle, you'll start shaping the foot by keeping 16 stitches at each end on a stitch holder, and knitting more rows on the centre stitches to form the top section of the foot.

KNITTING THE FOOT
The stitches for the foot section are held across two needles (51 stitches on each), as it's too bulky for them to fit on one needle. You use a third needle to do the actual knitting.

cross-stitch pillowcase

This is truly an heirloom piece to be handed down through the family. Be patient when you transfer the design and you will have a foolproof guide for your stitching.

Materials

1 pillowcase
1 skein DMC stranded embroidery
 cotton in each of the following
 colours:
  Very Light Dusty Rose (151)
  Very Dark Cranberry (600)
  Bright Chartreuse (704)
  Very Light Yellow Green (772)
  Medium Dark Rose (899)
  Medium Dark Raspberry (3832)
embroidery needle
20cm embroidery hoop (optional)
dressmaker's carbon and a sharp
 pencil

Method

1. Copy pattern (it's on the pattern sheet inside the back cover) to the fabric using carbon; we used pink and green for the separate areas. Use a tracing wheel and carbon to mark the position for the running stitch. Use a pencil and carbon to mark the position for the cross-stitch border and cross-stitch pattern.
2. Mount the top layer of the pillowcase in an embroidery hoop, if you are using one. If you are not using one, be especially careful to work your stitches through the top layer of the pillowcase only.
3. Stitch according to the pattern, using two strands of cotton in the colours indicated. See page 186 for instructions on cross stitch and blanket stitch.

TRANSFER THE DESIGN
The easiest way to transfer the design is to photocopy or trace the pattern, place a sheet of dressmaker's carbon between the design and the cloth, and trace over the design with a sharp pencil.

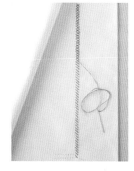

WORKING CROSS STITCH
Cross stitch may be worked in two ways: either as individual stitches or as two rows of slanted stitches. Use this second method for the cross-stitch border.

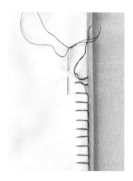

BLANKET STITCH EDGE
For the blanket stitch, try to keep the stitch heights even as you work. It will give a more accomplished look to the finished project.

stencilled pillowcase

This pillowcase looks magnificent, but if attempting an intricate stencil seems daunting, you could use the same techniques to complete a simpler design.

Materials

European pillowcase
firm white cardboard
3M Repositionable Spray Adhesive
stencil to fit pillowcase (We used Birds and Blossom panel JA121, available from the Stencil Gallery.)
Pebeo Setacolor Fabric Paint: Bengal Pink (22), Fawn (52), Aniseed Green (32), Cobalt Blue (11)
Pebeo Lightening Medium
stencil brushes
paper towel
low-tack masking tape (optional)
iron
clean paper or cloth

TIP

If you would like to stencil a matching set of pillowcases, simply reverse the stencil when you work on the other pillowcase. This will give you a mirror image.

Method

If you have never stencilled before, you may want to test your technique on calico first.

1. Launder the pillowcase to remove any starch or sizing, and iron.

2. Cut a piece of cardboard to fit snugly inside the pillowcase. Spray it with spray adhesive, insert into the pillowcase and position it behind the area to be stencilled. Smooth out any creases.

3. Apply a light coat of spray adhesive to the back of the stencil, then position it on the pillowcase. Press down firmly all over.

4. Have a look at the design and decide the order of work. If you need to mask any areas, use small pieces of low-tack masking tape. You can also use a piece of scrap card to mask small areas as you work.

5. Shake paints before use. Pick up a very small amount of paint on the end of the bristles and circle the brush vigorously on a wad of paper towel. Dab the brush on the towel until it is leaving only a very light, misty impression. Apply the paint through the holes in the stencil using a gentle circular motion. If you need more colour, apply a little more pressure or pick up more paint and dab it out onto paper towel again until the brush is almost dry and then apply to the stencil. Resist the temptation to load a lot of paint onto the brush.

6. Wash the brushes in hot, soapy water to clean. A brush must be absolutely dry before it is used again. To get a subtle blended effect, for instance, where brown stalks meld into green leaves, do not clean the brush between colours – simply pick up the new colour on top of the remnants of the old, dab onto paper towel and proceed.

7. The lightening medium can be used to blend a range of tones in the one colour, for instance, pink flowers that range from palest pink to a deep shade. Work with the lightest colour first, then gradually add more colour to the brush (always dabbing the excess onto paper towels) as you proceed.

8. When all the stencilling is finished, allow the paint to dry and then carefully lift away the stencil. Heat-set the paint with an iron, following the manufacturer's instructions.

Spraying a piece of cardboard with spray adhesive and slipping it into the pillowcase means the fabric is held fast and won't slip during the stencilling.

A light coating of spray adhesive will also keep the stencil in place. Press it down firmly on the pillowcase. Make sure there are no creases.

Lightening medium allows you to make subtle shades. Simply blend a little of the base colour into the lightening medium.

Apply the paint in a gentle circling motion. Never overload the brush, and circle it on a wad of paper towel first to remove any excess paint.

Let the paint dry before carefully lifting off the stencil. Do not remove the cardboard backing until the paint is completely dry.

Place clean paper or a cloth over the pattern when you heat-set the paint, to avoid scorching.

pillowcase with ribbons & beads

An absolute confection of ribbon and beads, this is a show pillowcase to be displayed on the bed rather than being used for sleeping. It would make anyone feel like a princess.

Materials

1 pillowcase
assorted ribbons, approximately
    60cm of each
4mm faceted beads (about 40)
seed beads (about 400)
small sewing needle
beading needle
sewing thread, in colours to match
    ribbons and pillowcase
seam ripper (unpicker)

Method

1. Lay out ribbons in the desired order across the pillowcase and cut to length, allowing 2.5cm extra length at each end.

2. Begin with the widest ribbon. Pin it to the pillowcase and, using a matching thread, stitch it in place with very small slip stitches along both edges. Begin and end the stitching 1cm from the bottom and top seams of the pillowcase, leaving 3.5cm of ribbon loose at each end. (Alternatively, machine stitch ribbon in place.)

3. Pin the next ribbon in place, approximately 6mm from the edge of the first. Stitch in place as before, stopping 1cm from the bottom and top seams of the pillowcase.

4. Continue to stitch the ribbons onto the pillowcase, working outwards in either direction from the first ribbon. When you get to the position for the first row of beads (the 4mm faceted beads), leave 12–15mm before adding the next ribbon. (Do not add beads until you have attached all the ribbon.)

5. Unpick the seams of the pillowcase where the ends of the ribbons lie. Tuck the ends of the ribbons inside the pillowcase and restitch the side seams to secure the ribbon ends. Finish slip stitching the ends of each ribbon to the pillowcase, so they are secured all the way to the seams.

6. Stitch the 4mm faceted beads, spacing them about 12mm apart. Use a beading needle and strong cotton thread that matches the pillowcase.

7. Stitch the seed beads in diagonal rows about 10–12 mm apart, placing beads about the same distance apart and staggering the beads in alternate rows. You can work by eye, as small deviations won't be noticeable.

DECIDE ON A DESIGN
Your first step is to decide on the arrangement of ribbons. Actually placing them on the pillowcase is the best way to do this.

STITCHING SEED BEADS
Use small running stitches to attach seed beads, and don't worry about keeping the rows perfectly straight. Use a beading needle as its very small eye passes easily through the beads' centres.

covered coathanger

Dressing your hangers with a padded cover makes them a better choice for delicate garments, coats and formal wear. And these look wonderful, too.

Materials

wooden coathanger with crossbar and
    removable metal hook
55cm fabric or 30cm each of two different
    fabrics (if you want to use a different
    fabric for the lining). Fabric should be
    at least 110cm wide.
polyester wadding
sewing thread
1 metre rickrack or bobble braid
30cm narrow ribbon, to cover hook
craft glue
large sheet of paper

JOINING THE PIECES
Stitch right around the outside
of the two shapes except
for a gap at the top for the
coathanger hook, and an 8cm
opening to turn the piece
right-side out.

Method

1. To make a pattern, lay your coathanger on a large piece of paper and trace around the shape. Add 2cm around the curved upper edges and 5cm along the straight lower edge. Cut out the paper pattern on the outer lines.

2. Using your pattern, trace and cut four pieces of fabric: two will be used for the lining, so if you'd like to have a lining different from the outer cover, cut two shapes from each of two fabrics. Also cut two shapes from wadding.

3. Baste a wadding shape to the wrong side of each of the two outer fabric shapes, using tacking stitches around the outer edges. (Don't skip this step – it is difficult to keep the wadding in place when sewing if you don't baste it first.)

4. Match a lining shape to each outer shape, right sides together. Using a 1.5cm seam, pin then stitch across the lower straight edge. Trim the wadding close to the seam to reduce bulk.

5. Match the two shapes, right sides together and all edges even. Using a 1.5cm seam, pin and stitch the two shapes together right around the outer edge: leave a 1cm opening at the top of the curved edge on both the outer cover and lining for the hook, and leave an 8cm opening in one section of the lining seam (see photo).

6. Trim the wadding close to the seam, then turn the cover right side out through the opening in the lining seam. Slip stitch the opening closed. Push lining up into the cover and press. Remove tacking.

7. Stitch rickrack or braid to lower edge of cover – not only is this decorative, it also stops the lower seam from rolling out.

8. Unscrew the hook from the hanger. To finish the hook, use a dab of craft glue on one end of the ribbon and hold it in place about 1cm from the curved end until secure. Wind the ribbon evenly around the hook to cover. Start by winding back over the raw end towards the end of the hook to conceal it; then wind to the bottom of the hook and secure the end with a little craft glue.

9. Carefully insert hook through the opening and screw into the hanger. Slip the cover over coathanger.

laundry bag

A laundry bag neatly stows your washing while you're travelling. This one, with its cute little clothesline, will become the first thing you pack.

Materials

1 piece of fabric 50cm x 1.5 metres
scraps of fabric for appliqué
3 metres piping cord
sewing thread to match bag fabric
machine embroidery thread to match
   appliqué scraps
DMC stranded embroidery cotton
   in Light Drab Brown (612) and
   Very Light Topaz (727)
embroidery needle
fusible web (such as HeatnBond)
water-erasable fabric marking pen or pencil

PLACING APPLIQUE
The shapes for the clothes should first be drawn and roughly cut out of the fusible web. After fusing the shapes to the fabric scraps, trim to the final shape and arrange on the bag before fusing in place.

Method

1. Fold fabric in half to yield a rectangle 75cm x 50cm. Draw a line across the width of the fabric 25cm from the fold, for the clothesline.
2. Embroider the clothesline by hand, working chain stitch in three strands of Very Light Topaz (727).
3. Trace shapes for clothes (see page 178) onto the paper side of the fusible web. Cut around the shapes roughly – about 1cm outside the lines. Place the fusible web shapes on to the wrong side of the fabric scraps with the paper side facing up and fuse them in place, following the manufacturer's directions. Cut out each of the shapes on the traced lines.
4. Remove the backing paper from the shapes and place them on the fabric just below the stitched clothesline. When in desired position, fuse them in place.
5. Using a sewing machine threaded with machine embroidery thread, satin stitch around the outside of the shapes.
6. Embroider pegs at the top of each shape by hand, working straight stitch in three strands of Light Drab Brown (612).
7. Turn under a 5cm hem on each short end of the fabric. Pin, then stitch in place. Leave the sides of the hems unstitched, to act as the casing for the drawstring.
8. Fold fabric in half, right sides together. Using a 5mm seam, pin then stitch the sides of the bag. Turn the bag right side out.
9. Cut the piping cord in half. Thread one length through a hem pocket, across the bag, out the other side, and then back through the other hem pocket. Repeat with the second length, starting from the opposite side of the bag. Knot the ends of each cord together.

garment bag

Protect your special items with their own garment bag. Natural fabrics such as cotton are best to use, as they allow garments to breathe.

Materials

1.25 metres x 120cm-wide fabric. If you wish to use fabric that is only 112cm wide or if you wish to cut the bag so that the printed design runs the length of the bag (as with the striped bag), you will need to purchase 2.5 metres of fabric.

1.2 metre zipper (buy a roll of continuous zipper, and cut the length you need)

7 metres contrasting bias binding

sewing thread to match

wooden coathanger

tailor's chalk or a soft pencil

Method

1. From the fabric cut one rectangle 56cm x 120cm for the back and two rectangles 30cm x 120cm for the front.

2. Match one long edge of the zipper with one long edge of a front rectangle, wrong sides together. Pin, baste and then stitch using a narrow zigzag stitch. Repeat with other edge of the zipper on the other front piece. You'll have exposed seams on each side of the zipper. Press.

3. Cover raw edges of each seam with 120cm bias binding (see below).

4. Make a loop using 12cm bias binding folded in half and stitched along the edge. Pin, then baste at the base of the zipper.

5. With wrong sides facing, pin the bag's front and back together. Stitch along the bottom edge using a narrow zigzag stitch, catching the ends of the loop. Cover raw edges of the seam with bias binding.

6. To shape the top of the bag, lay it flat on a table. Place a coathanger across the top and trace along its top edge, extending the line out to the fabric's edge. Cut both layers of fabric on the curved line.

7. Pin, then stitch the sides and top of the bag using a narrow zigzag stitch. Cover raw edges with bias binding, turning under 1cm of bias binding at the beginning and end of your stitching for a neat finish.

8. Open the zipper, insert the hanger and zip the bag closed.

ADDING THE LOOP

Place the loop so that its top points to the top of the bag. Its ends will be held in place by the outside line of stitching.

SHAPING THE TOP

After you have joined the bag at its bottom, you can then shape its top. Mark around the hanger's curved edge with tailor's chalk or a pencil.

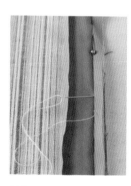

ADDING BIAS BINDING

To attach the bias binding, unfold one edge and pin then tack it to the seam, with the fold in line with the bottom of the zigzag stitch.

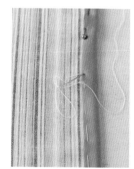

FINISHING BIAS BINDING

Fold the other edge of the bias binding over the raw edge and to the other side. Pin, then tack in place, so that it covers the zigzag stitch. Using a straight stitch, stitch in place.

shoe bag

Perfect for travelling, or for just keeping your shoes nice, our shoe bag has an internal panel so your shoes fit snugly, one on each side. You can also add a braid tag to easily identify your shoes.

Materials

50cm of fabric (at least 110cm wide)
matching thread
braid for tag (optional)
1.3 metres of cord
safety pin (to thread cord)

Method

1. Cut two rectangles 32cm x 44cm for the outer bag. Cut a rectangle 32cm x 38cm for the internal panel.

2. Double fold a 1cm hem on one short edge of the internal panel. (This will be the top edge.) Pin, then machine stitch in place.

3. Match the two rectangles for the outer bag, right sides together. Place internal panel on top, with its bottom and side edges matching the outer bag panels. If you are adding a braid tag, fold an 8cm strip of braid in half and pin in place on one long edge, raw edges matching.

4. Pin and machine stitch the panels together, using a 1.5cm seam: start stitching at the top edge of the inner panel, stitch down one long side of the bag, across the bottom, and back up the other side to the top edge of the inner panel. Finish seam edges.

5. Just above the inner panel, snip the outer bag panels from their outside edges to the seam line. Fold raw edges under 1cm; press in place. Stitch 5mm in from the folded edge to hold the hem in place (see diagram below).

6. To make the casing for the drawstring, fold the top edge of each outer panel over 1cm and press. Fold over another 3cm, so the bottom edge of the hems sits just above the top edge of the inner panel. Pin, then stitch in place. Turn the bag right side out.

7. Cut cord in half. Thread one length through both casings. Repeat with the second length, starting from the opposite side of the bag. Knot ends of each cord together.

NOTE

If you are using a heavy fabric such as velvet for the bag, make the internal panel from a lighter weight fabric. You will need a 40cm length for the internal panel, and a 50cm length for the outside panels.

ADDING THE CORDS

There are actually two pieces of cord threaded through the casing from opposite sides. A large safety pin put in the cord's end makes it easy to thread.

INTERNAL PANEL

The internal panel can be in the same fabric or in a contrasting material.

BRAID TAG

A braid tag is an easy way to identify whose shoes are in which bag. It's a practical idea if you have made several bags in the same fabric.

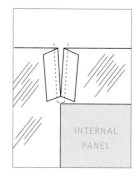

FORMING THE CASING

Just above the top of the internal panel, snip the side seams from the outer edge to the stitching line. Fold the seam's raw edges under, then stitch right around the opening.

picnic set

This matching set of a picnic rug, two cushions and napkins is a gift for someone to treasure.

Materials

2.2 metres x 150cm-wide heavyweight variegated red fabric (rug front)

1.7 metres x 150cm-wide waterproof fabric (rug back)

sewing thread to match main fabric

dressmaker's carbon

DMC Perle cotton #5. We used Peacock Blue (807) and Light Parrot Green (907).

5 metres bias binding in colour to match rug fabric

2 cushion inserts 30cm x 40cm (breakfast cushion size)

embroidery needle

CROSS STITCH
The cross stitch helps hold the black waterproof backing to the front of the rug. For a neat finish on the back, keep the knotted ends of thread between the two layers.

Method

1. Cut a 170cm length from the heavyweight red fabric for the front of the rug. The remaining fabric will be used for the cushions.

2. Mark the positions for the cross stitches on the red fabric, starting at the centre. We worked stitches about 15mm high in straight rows about 15cm apart.

3. Match the rug and the backing fabrics, raw edges matching and wrong sides together, and pin.

4. Work cross stitches in Light Parrot Green (907) through both layers. For a neat finish, start and end each stitch between the two fabric layers: to do this knot the end of the thread, insert the needle about 10mm from the cross, exiting at the base of the cross, and tug the knot gently through the rug fabric. Before completing the second diagonal in each cross stitch, knot the thread about 23mm from the beginning of the stitch. Make the stitch, tugging gently to pull the knot through the rug fabric, but not all the way through to the back of the rug.

5. Make a light mark on the long edges of the rug, 5cm from each corner. Turn under 2.5cm on the waterproof backing fabric on each of its short sides. Then turn these hems under again. Top stitch the hems in place using thread to match the front of the rug.

6. If necessary, trim the long edges of the rug front and back so that they are even, and finish with bias binding. To attach the bias binding, unfold one long edge and pin it in place so that it matches the raw edge of the rug front. Turn under the first 1cm of bias binding neatly, so that the folded end is even with the edge of the rug. Baste to hold in place. Fold the other long edge of the bias binding over the raw edges and to the back of the rug. Pin, then machine stitch in place. Remove basting.

7. Remove threads from the short ends of the rug front to make a fringe 5cm long.

napkins

Materials

white napkins at least 45cm square. (We
used napkins that were 50cm square.)
DMC stranded embroidery cotton. We used
Turquoise (597), Light Parrot Green (907)
and Dark Raspberry (3831).
dressmakers' carbon
embroidery needle

Method

1. Mark the position for the embroidery using dressmakers' carbon,
referring to the pattern on the pattern sheet inside the back cover.
2. Work the inner and outer rows of running stitch in Light Parrot
Green (907), and adjacent rows in Turquoise (597). Work cross stitch in
Dark Raspberry (3831). Use two strands of thread for all the stitching.

cushions

Materials

refer to the Materials list on
the previous page

Method

1. Cut two rectangles 46cm x 70cm from the remaining heavyweight
red fabric.
2. On each rectangle, mark the position for a line of running stitch
6cm from each long edge.
3. Work a line of running stitch using Peacock Blue (807).
4. Work cross stitch in Light Parrot Green (907) and another row of
running stitch in Peacock Blue, as shown in picture.
5. Bind the two short edges of each rectangle with bias binding, as
you did with the rug.
6. Lay the rectangle on a table, with the embroidered side face down.
Fold the top short edge over 19cm towards the centre of the fabric,
and pin to hold in place. Fold the bottom short edge over 20cm
– it will overlap the fabric from the first fold – and pin to hold. The
cushion cover will now measure 30cm x 46cm.
7. Stitch along the 30cm sides, 3cm from each raw edge. Remove
threads to make a fringe. Put the cushion inserts inside each cover.

FOLDING THE COVER

To form the cushion cover,
fold over one short edge
of the cushion by 19cm, and
the other by 20cm. This
will make a rectangle with
an overlap at the back.

FRINGING

To do the fringing, remove
threads to near the line of
topstitching. Using an awl, a
knitting needle, or the closed
tip of a small pair of sharp
scissors makes it easier.

EASY ALTERNATIVE

You will need to make up the rug
and cushion covers in a sturdy fabric.
We used a colourful tweed woven
in Scotland. Alternatively, you could
buy a woollen travel rug, then make
up the cushions and napkins in
a complementary colour to create a
picnicking set.

cutlery roll

Pop your cutlery for a picnic in this bright roll made from a tea-towel. It keeps sharp edges covered and everything in its place. It's also brilliantly easy to wash.

Materials

tea-towel (51cm x 69cm)
fade-out marking pen
sewing thread to match the tea-towel
1 metre of 1cm wide satin ribbon

Method

1. Press tea-towel. Turn up 15cm along one long edge, wrong sides together, and press. At each end, stitch the outer edges together, as close to the edge as possible.

2. Use a fade-out marking pen to rule a number of evenly spaced vertical lines across the pocket, creating individual pockets for cutlery. We marked out 12 x 5cm pockets with one larger pocket at one end.

3. Stitch along the ruled lines, working back stitches at the start and finish of each seam to finish off the thread. Trim threads. Do not press the pockets until the marker has faded. (This can take up to 24 hours. Marker can also be gently washed out.)

4. Fold ribbon in half and crease. Position the ribbon on the outside of the roll, so that the crease is 5mm from one edge and 3cm from the top of the pocket. Stitch in place using a close, narrow zigzag across the width of the ribbon. Cut ends of ribbon on the diagonal to prevent fraying. Insert cutlery, roll up and tie with ribbon to secure.

MAKE A SET
You can keep eating utensils in one cutlery roll, and cooking kit in another. Use tea-towels with different patterns so it's easy to identify the bundles.

CUSTOMISE POCKETS
We marked out pockets to fit standard cutlery pieces, but you can adapt the design to fit larger utensils like tongs or serving spoons.

TIP
This cutlery holder is a neat way to cart utensils outdoors, and when the time comes to clean up you can quickly spot if anything's missing. An empty pocket means a piece of cutlery needs tracking down.

table linen with lacy doilies

A store-bought table runner and napkin set is made pretty with doilies and easy embroidery. The key is to keep it simple.

Materials

plain table runner
4 napkins to match the table runner
cotton lace to edge the table runner
6 circular crocheted lace doilies, with
  a diameter of 10cm
sewing thread to match
2 skeins of stranded embroidery thread
  in a contrasting colour
embroidery needle

Method

1. Pin, then machine stitch lace around the edge of the table runner. Start and finish in one corner, turning under raw edges neatly.
2. Pin, then tack, a doily in position at each end of the table runner and in one corner of each napkin, referring to the photograph for guidance with position. Machine stitch in place.
3. Using three strands of the contrasting embroidery thread, work running stitch 5mm from the edge on all sides of the table runner and napkins.
4. Using six strands, work stitches through the doilies to highlight their design, securing the thread neatly on the back.

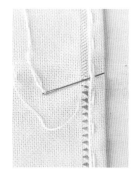

DRAWN THREAD WORK
Working on the wrong side, pull through the embroidery cotton at the bottom of the drawn section. Pick up four of the exposed vertical threads with the needle.

FINISHING THE WORK
Pull the needle through and pick up two horizontal threads on the hem. Make sure the same two horizontal threads are picked up all along.

DRAWN THREAD WORK

Our table runner and napkins were bought with the drawn thread border already done. To do it yourself, first find the centre point of each side, about 4cm in from the edge. Using a needle, carefully lift one horizontal thread at the centre and snip with scissors. With the needle, gently remove the thread, working from the centre out to the corners. Repeat with the two adjacent threads. Leave the thread ends long enough so you can darn them back into the fabric.

To work the hem stitch, use the contrasting stranded embroidery cotton; if you are working on linen, use three or four strands; for a lighter fabric, such as organdie or lawn, use one or two strands. Working on the wrong side, from left to right, pull through the embroidery cotton at the bottom of the drawn section. Place the needle in from the right and pick up four of the exposed vertical threads. Pull the needle through and pick up two horizontal threads below (see photo). Continue, making sure the same two horizontal threads below are picked up all along.

ribbon-trimmed table linen

A strip of ribbon turns this table setting into something special. Use a graphic ribbon like ours for a modern look, or choose a plain satin for a traditional effect.

Materials

plain coloured table runner
4 napkins in a contrasting colour
sewing cotton to match table runner and
    napkins
1cm wide patterned ribbon for trim (we
    used 5 metres)
seam ripper, scalpel or small sharp scissors
disappearing (fade-out) marking pen

Method

1. Mark pairs of buttonholes, 1cm apart, at 5cm intervals along both sides of table runner. At each end of the runner, mark a single buttonhole, not a pair. The buttonholes should be 3–4mm wider than the ribbon and end 2cm from the edge of the table runner.

2. In the same way, mark pairs of buttonholes along one side of each napkin with fade-out marking pen.

3. Machine stitch buttonholes in thread to match table runner and napkins. Carefully open up each buttonhole with a seam ripper, a sharp scalpel or a pair of scissors.

4. Thread ribbon through buttonholes. An easy way to do this is to insert a safety pin at one end of the ribbon, and then push the safety pin up and down through the buttonholes along the length of the table runner and napkins. Trim the ribbon and secure at each end with a few stitches worked by hand in the hem on the wrong side of the fabric, so that the stitches don't show on the front.

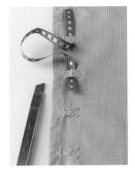

CUTTING BUTTONHOLES

Using a sharp blade, such as a scalpel or Stanley knife, allows good control when you cut the fabric inside the buttonholes. A seam ripper also works well.

BUTTONHOLES

A machine-sewn buttonhole has two parallel rows of sewing in a narrow zigzag stitch, with the ends finished in a broader zigzag stitch.

To work out the buttonhole's size, measure the button's width plus its thickness, and add 3mm.

Use fade-out marking pen to mark the fabric with the position of each buttonhole opening and its ends. Take care the marks are directly on the fabric's grain. Extend the marks so you can see them while you're stitching.

sewing kit

A small sewing kit, filled with essentials, is a useful bit of equipment for anyone. This kit can be packed for trips away or stowed in a drawer to be used at home.

Materials

2 pieces of fabric 10cm x 26cm, one for outside and one for lining
1 piece of tablecloth plastic 8cm x 26cm
1 metre satin bias binding, 25mm wide
50cm cord
1 button
notions to fill pockets: embroidery thread bobbins with sewing threads in a variety of shades, spare buttons, needles, pins, safety pins, folding scissors
non-permanent marking pen

Method

1. Lay the plastic over pattern printed on page 176. Trace pattern on plastic using a non-permanent marker. Cut out plastic shape. Place shape on right side of lining fabric, bottom and side edges matching.
2. Machine three rows of stitching where indicated on the pattern, from the bottom edge to a point 3mm above the plastic's top edge.
3. Match fabric for the outside with the lining, wrong sides together. Pin, then stitch around sides using a narrow zigzag stitch.
4. Finish raw edges with bias binding. Starting at one corner, pin, then baste binding in place around edges. To mitre the corners, fold the bias binding up and away from the sewing kit, creating a diagonal fold. Hold the fold in place and bring the binding in line with the next edge of the kit. As you near the end of the fourth edge, trim binding 1cm longer than needed. Fold cut ends under and stitch in place. (See page 28 for more on bias binding.)
5. Fold binding over, on to the lining. Pin, then machine stitch in place using thread to match the binding. Remove basting.
6. Lay out sewing kit lining side up. Fold right-hand edge to the middle. Fold kit again, on the centre line of stitching, then fold left edge over and press firmly. Pin, then sew one end of the cord in place, referring to the photo for guidance. Knot the cord's other end. Mark position for button 3cm to the left of the cord and sew it on.
7. Fill pockets with notions. Fold kit up and secure by winding the cord around and then looping it around the button.

ESSENTIAL GEAR
Stock the sewing kit with needles, safety pins and thread wrapped around little holders, which may be bought from sewing and craft stores. Also include a small pair of scissors in the kit.

TIP
To stop the plastic slipping when you stitch it, either lay greaseproof paper on top, or give it a light dusting of talcum powder and use a walking foot on the sewing machine.

appliquéd throw rug

Personalise a throw rug with a scatter of snoozy letters.
It's perfect on a winter's night in front of the television.

Materials

1 purchased throw rug
25cm square of felt
machine embroidery thread in colour
   to match felt
heavy-duty fusible web such as
   HeatnBond Ultrahold
computer and printer (optional)

Method

1. Using a computer, print a letter 'Z' in a large size, such as 72 point. Our letters are in Cooper Black font. Alternatively, hand draw a 'Z'.
2. Photocopy the letter five times; use the Enlarge function to produce letters in a variety of sizes.
3. Trace each Z from the back of the photocopied pages onto the paper side of the heavy-duty fusible web. That is, you need to trace the Z in reverse.
4. Cut around the five reverse-Z shapes roughly – about 1cm outside the lines. Place the fusible web shapes on the felt with the paper side facing up and fuse them in place, following the manufacturer's directions. Cut out each of the five Z shapes on the traced lines.
5. Remove the backing paper from each shape and place them on the throw rug. When in desired position, fuse them in place.
6. Using a sewing machine threaded with machine embroidery thread, satin stitch (a close zigzag stitch) around the letters.

SEWING THE Zs

Although felt does not fray, it is still best to use fusible web. As well as making it easier to cut the shape, it ensures the motif stays in place while you sew it.

TIPS

At the beginning of each line of stitching, backstitch five or six stitches to lock the threads in place before zigzagging. Do the same at the end of the zigzagging.
When turning corners, leave the needle in the fabric on the outside edge of the design, lift the presser foot and pivot fabric as required.

knitted scarf

Even a novice knitter could attempt this gorgeous scarf. There is nothing tricky, just beautiful wool made into a luscious garment.

Materials

5 balls (50g each) of Freedom 100% wool in Cream (401) by Twilleys of Stamford
5 balls (50g each) of Emotive by Sensual in Colour 14 (blue)
1 pair 10mm knitting needles
1 crochet hook (optional) to make fringe

Method

1. Working both colours together, cast on 23 stitches.
2. 1st row: K2 * P1 K1 repeat from* to last stitch, K1.
2nd row: K1 P1 to last stitch, K1.
Note that always knitting, rather than purling, the last stitch in the row stops the scarf's edges from rolling. Repeat rows 1 and 2 until the scarf measures 148cm long. (Its width is approximately 24cm.)
3. Cast off loosely in rib (K1, P1) using blue yarn only. Break off yarn and finish off.
4. To make the fringe, cut 15 x 45cm lengths of blue yarn and 28 x 45cm lengths of cream yarn. Attach evenly across one end of the scarf by folding yarn in half and using the crochet hook to pull through the ends to make a knot with each strand. (See page 185 for more instructions on making the fringe.) We alternated our strands, using both yarns in one strand, then using the cream yarn on its own on the next strand and so on. Repeat on the other end, using the same number of strands to make the fringe.

THE FRINGE

A deep fringe adds to the cuddliness of the scarf. Allow an entire ball of wool just for the fringe.

ALTERNATIVE

Instead of using two colours at once, this scarf may be worked with a single yarn, though it will look looser.
The scarf could be striped by changing the wool every 10cm to eventually give 15 stripes. You could also make uneven stripes, but work out a pattern before you start knitting. You could copy the design from a striped piece of fabric.

flowery crocheted scarf

This is a retro-style scarf for girls of all ages. After doing a couple of flowers, you'll discover just how simple crochet is.

Materials

No.3 crochet hook

2 balls (50g each) mohair in Citrus

1 ball (50g) Jo Sharp Soho Summer DK Cotton in Orchid (Colour 214)

1 ball (50g) Jo Sharp Soho Summer DK Cotton in Calico (Colour 228)

2 balls (25g each) 4ply Heirloom Baby Wool in pink

2 balls (25g each) 4ply Heirloom Baby Wool in blue

2 balls (50g each) Sunbeam Paris Mohair in Snow White (Shade 1101) (most of one of the balls is used for the fringe)

Method

1. See next page for colour combinations. With the centre colour work 4ch, then join into a circle with a ss into the first ch.

Round 1: 1ch, work 15dc into the circle, then ss to first ch.

Round 2: 3ch, *miss 1dc, 1tr into next dc, 1ch, repeat from * six more times. Join with a ss into second of 3ch.

Round 3: Join 1st contrast colour into top of last stitch with a ss, 1ch, into ch space work 1tr, 1dtr, 1tr, 1dc to form a petal, *into next ch space work 1dc, 1tr, 1dtr, 1tr, 1dc, repeat from * until eight petals have been worked. Join to first petal with a ss.

Round 4: Join 2nd contrast colour with a ss between dc of last and first petal to begin the second row of petals, 4ch, *1dc between dc at start of next petal, 3ch, repeat from * to end. Join with a ss into the first of 4ch.

Round 5: 1ch, into first 3ch space work 1tr , 2dtr, 1tr, 1dc, *into next 3ch space work 1dc, 1tr, 2dtr, 1tr, 1dc, repeat from * until eight petals have been worked. Join to first petal with a ss.

Round 6: Join 3rd contrast colour with a ss between dc of last and first petal of second row of petals, 5ch, *1dc between dc at start of next petal, 4ch, repeat from * to end of round. Join with ss into first ch.

Round 7: 1ch, into first 4ch space work 1tr, 3dtr, 1tr, 1dc, *into next ch space work 1dc, 1tr, 3dtr, 1tr, 1dc, repeat from * until eight petals have been worked. Join to first petal with a ss. Break off yarn, draw the end through the loop on the hook and pull up to fasten tightly.

2. Darn in the ends of yarn neatly at the back of the work. Arrange flowers in 16 rows of two flowers each, with different colour combinations next to each other.

3. Flowers may be joined with a few stitches in wool at the peaks of the outside petals. More experienced crocheters could join the flowers together by passing a loop through the petal of an adjacent flower while working the double treble in the final round.

4. To make the fringe, cut 54 x 45cm lengths of yarn (we used the white mohair). Divide them into nine bundles of six strands each. Attach the bundles evenly across one end of the scarf by doubling to make a knot for each strand. Repeat on the other end, using the same number of strands to make the fringe. Trim the fringe so the ends are even. (See page 185 for more on making fringes.)

KEY
ch = chain stitch
ss = slip stitch
dc = double crochet
tr = treble
dtr = double treble

Colour combinations

This scarf uses flowers in four colour combinations. Make eight of each for a total of 32 flowers.

	COMBINATION A	COMBINATION B	COMBINATION C	COMBINATION D
CENTRE	blue baby wool	calico cotton	citrus mohair	orchid cotton
FIRST ROUND	calico cotton	blue baby wool	orchid cotton	pink baby wool
SECOND ROUND	snow white mohair	pink baby wool	pink baby wool	blue baby wool
THIRD ROUND	orchid cotton	citrus mohair	blue baby wool	snow white mohair

You form the petals in Round 3 by working treble and double treble into the spaces on the previous row.

In Round 4, you crochet a row of chain stitches that will be the foundation for the next row of petals.

The larger petals in Round 5 are worked on the row of chain stitch made in the previous round.

EASY ALTERNATIVE

The scarf shown here uses a mix of mohair, cotton knit and 4ply baby wool. However if you're not experienced at crochet, it will be much easier to do this project with a selection of plain 4ply or 5ply wools. You could also reduce the number of colour combinations.

sequined singlet

Stitch this divine silver flower on a singlet as a gift for a house guest. It's easier to do than it looks. You could also repeat the pattern to embellish a cushion.

Materials

singlet top
60cm small silver sequin trim
20 green bugle beads
30 small silver beads
natural-colour cotton thread
super fine needle

Method

1. Transfer flower pattern from page 176 to the singlet using dressmaker's carbon or a soft pencil.

2. Hand-stitch silver sequin trim in place over the outline of the flower, using a running stitch worked through the sequins. Cut trim at the end of each petal and secure with a knot. You may lose a few sequins off the trim when it's cut; save these for the flower's centre.

3. Using a super fine needle, stitch clusters (rather than a single circle) of the silver beads at the base of each petal. Use the beads to hide the ends of the silver sequins.

4. Stitch bugle beads in a circle inside the silver beads, referring to the photograph for guidance.

5. For the centre of the flower, use a combination of sequins and small silver beads as shown in the photo below. You will need five or six sequins and beads.

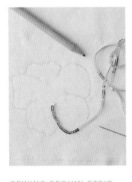

SEWING SEQUIN STRIP
Use running stitch to attach the sequin strip, passing the needle through the centre of the sequins.

THE FLOWER'S CENTRE
To sew sequins in the flower's centre, do a backstitch, then pull the thread through the sequin, then a seed bead, then back through the sequin. Finish with a backstitch.

BUGLE BEADS
Attaching the bugle beads is simple. Just do a backstitch, pull the needle and thread through the bead, and do another backstitch.

table linen with suffolk puff flowers

What could be sweeter for a summer setting? We have turned traditional Suffolk puffs into flowers, and the effect is as fresh as a daisy.

Materials

plain coloured table runner (main colour), ours measures 33cm x 156cm

4 napkins in a contrasting colour

2 skeins stranded embroidery thread in main colour

1 skein stranded embroidery thread in contrast colour

15cm of 90cm wide floral cotton fabric for table runner Suffolk puffs

15cm of 90cm wide floral cotton fabric for napkin Suffolk puffs

10 buttons (approx 1.5cm wide)

soft pencil or tailor's chalk

compass

Method

1. Mark the embroidery design (it's on the pattern sheet inside the back cover) on the napkins and table runner with a soft pencil or tailor's chalk. At its closest point, the design should be approximately 4cm from the edges of the table runner and 2cm from the edges of the napkins.

2. Work the design in running stitch on the napkins using six strands of the main colour thread. You could also work it in stem stitch.

3. Work the design in running stitch on the table runner using six strands of the contrast colour thread.

4. To make the Suffolk puffs, draw 12cm diameter circles on the floral fabrics using the compass. You will need six Suffolk puffs cut from one fabric for the table runner and four cut from the other fabric for the napkins. Cut the circles out on the lines.

5. Fold over a 5mm hem around the edge of each circle and work running stitch close to the fold. Leave the thread tails loose at the beginning and end of your stitching. Pull up the thread to gather circles tightly (hems inside) and tie off the threads securely. Flatten the Suffolk puffs so that the gathers sit neatly in the centre.

6. Pin Suffolk puffs in position on table runner and napkins, referring to the photograph for guidance. Place a button over the middle of the gathered side on each Suffolk puff and stitch in place.

SUFFOLK PUFFS
To make the puffs, fold over a 5mm hem all around the edge of the circle. Hand-sew a line of running stitch close to the fold, then pull the ends of the thread to gather the puff.

FINISHING THE PUFFS
Tie off the gathering thread and flatten the puffs. Pin in position and sew a button over the centre.

voile tablecloth

This is a cloth for a special occasion. It is light and delicate, with seam detailing and a simple row of mother-of-pearl buttons.

Materials

5 metres 1500cm-wide white cotton voile
white sewing cotton
20mm shell buttons (40 in total)
stranded embroidery cotton in off-white
  (use Anchor stranded cotton in
  Colour 926 or DMC stranded embroidery
  cotton in Ecru)
embroidery needle
tailor's chalk (optional)

Method

1. Cut one rectangle 95cm x 226cm and two rectangles 53cm x 226cm from the voile.
2. With wrong sides together, and allowing a 6mm seam, pin and stitch the narrow rectangles to the left and right long edges of the wider rectangle.
3. Trim the seam edges back to 3mm and press them to one side. Fold the fabric along the stitched seams, this time with right sides together. Pin and stitch a 6mm seam. This will create a french seam, enclosing the raw edges of the first seam inside the allowance.
4. Press both seams towards the outer edge of the tablecloth. Measure 52.5cm from both ends of the tablecloth and fold the fabric with right sides together along these lines (at right angles to the existing french seams). Pin along the fold.
5. Stitch a 6mm seam along the fold line to create a false french seam. Press the seam allowance towards the ends of the tablecloth.
6. Top stitch along the outer edges of all of the seams so they sit flat when on the table.
7. Fold and press a double 6mm hem around all four edges of the tablecloth. Machine stitch 4mm from the edge of the hem.
8. Use tailor's chalk or a line of basting to mark a line on the side and end border sections, 17cm from the french seam. Measure 5cm along this line from the side french seam and mark a point for the first button. Mark further button positions every 10cm.
9. Stitch a shell button at each marked point, using three strands of embroidery cotton.
10. Press the tablecloth carefully, ensuring french seams are pressed towards the hems.

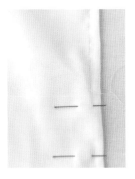

MAKING FRENCH SEAMS
Place wrong sides of fabric together and stitch. Trim back the seam allowance to 3mm, fold fabric back, pin in place and do another row of stitching 6mm from the fold. This encloses the first seam's edges.

TOP STITCHING
Top stitching along the edges of all the seams makes them lie flat and also gives a decorative finish.

FRENCH SEAM
A french seam is a double seam that encloses the raw edges of the fabric inside the seam allowance, preventing any fraying. It's particularly suitable for sheer fabrics such as voile, lawn and silk, where seams may be seen through the fabric. Here the seams are used as a feature.

table linen with panels

Add some colour and pattern to your table with this elegant runner and napkin set.

table runner

Materials

1.3 metres of floral fabric (at least 110cm wide)

1.3 metres of plain fabric (at least 90cm wide)

15cm of gingham (at least 110cm wide)

7.5 metres of fringe or braiding to match floral fabric

sewing thread to match fringe or braiding

Method

1. Cut a rectangle 21cm x 127cm from the plain fabric. Cut two rectangles 9cm x 127cm and two rectangles 9cm x 21cm from the floral fabric. Cut four squares 9cm x 9cm from the gingham.

2. Stitch a gingham square to each end of the short floral rectangles. Finish seam edges with zigzag stitch.

3. Stitch the long floral strips to the long sides of the plain fabric rectangle. Finish seam edges.

4. Stitch the shorter strips across the ends of the long rectangle, lining up the cross seams. Finish seam edges.

5. Turn under, pin, then stitch a 1.5cm hem on edges of the runner.

6. Position fringing over the seams, then pin and tack in place. Machine stitch in place.

napkin

Method

1. To make four napkins, cut eight rectangles 9cm x 40cm from the plain fabric. Cut four squares 40cm x 40cm from the floral fabric. Cut four squares 9cm x 9cm from the gingham.

2. Stitch a plain strip to one edge of each floral square.

3. Stitch a gingham square to one end of the remaining four plain rectangles. Finish seam edges.

4. Stitch the two pieces together, lining up the cross seams. Finish seam edges. Turn under, pin, then stitch a 1.5cm hem on all four edges of the napkins.

5. Position fringing over the seams, then pin and tack in place. Machine stitch in place.

JOINING PANELS
It's important to line up the seams when joining the panels on this project. Pinning, then tacking them in place before machine stitching will help.

BRAID FRINGING
As well as giving the runner a nicely trimmed finish, the braid will disguise any seams that are not quite straight.

NOTE
Choose fabrics of a similar weight, as this makes them easier to work with. Use a 5mm seam throughout this project unless otherwise noted.

beaded covers for jugs

These bring back childhood memories of afternoon tea with nanna, when the jug of milk and bowls of jam and cream were draped with pretty beaded doilies.

Materials

vintage lace doilies (we used a square doily, a round doily and a scalloped doily)

narrow satin ribbons, various colours and widths

silver pearls, large (round doily)

silver pearls, large, medium and small (square doily)

silver seed beads (square doily)

seed beads in a colour to match the ribbon (scalloped doily)

faceted rocailles, 3mm, in a colour to match the ribbon (scalloped doily)

teardrop beads in a colour to match the ribbon (scalloped doily)

needle and sewing thread to match ribbons

beading needle and beading thread

clear nail varnish (optional)

Method

1. Select ribbons of appropriate widths for the open spaces in the lace doily you have chosen. Weave the ribbon through the open spaces, threading it loosely so the doily still lies flat. You may need to work some small stitches on the inner edge of the ribbon so that it sits flat against the doily, particularly if the ribbon is wider than 5mm. Leave short tails of ribbon, about 5cm long, to cross over. Secure the ribbons at the cross-over point with a few tiny stitches.

2. Using a beading needle and thread, attach beads to the edges of the doily. Choose solid glass beads that will weigh the edge of the doily down.

3. For the square doily: Begin at one corner of the doily. Stitch the beading thread into the edge of the lace to hide the tail of thread, and bring the thread out at the corner. Thread on one small silver pearl, one medium silver pearl and one large silver pearl, followed by a seed bead. Take the beading needle back through the pearl beads, then stitch a couple of times into the corner of the lace to secure this drop. Thread on two small silver pearls, one medium silver pearl and one large silver pearl, followed by a seed bead, as before. Take the needle back through the pearls and secure the thread in the corner of the lace. Thread on one small silver pearl, one medium silver pearl and one large silver pearl plus a seed bead. Take the needle back through the pearls to the corner of the lace and stitch to secure. Stitch the beading thread to hide it in the edge of the lace and snip off the thread. Repeat at other corners.

4. For the round doily: Stitch the beading thread into the edge of the lace, leaving a 5cm tail of thread. Pass the thread through a large silver pearl and stitch through the edge of the lace before passing the thread through the pearl again in the same direction. Stitch into the edge of the lace and tie the ends of the beading thread into a secure knot. Snip off the ends of the thread close to the knot. You could add a dab of clear nail varnish to prevent the knot coming undone. Repeat at regular intervals around the edge of the doily.

5. For the scalloped doily: Work as for the round doily. At the bottom of each scallop, add a seed bead, a faceted rocaille and a teardrop bead, passing the beading thread back through the rocaille and seed bead. Fasten the ends of the beading thread as before.

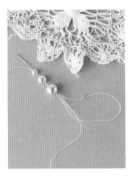

A DROP OF PEARLS
Work a few stitches in the doily to secure the thread, then thread on the silver pearls and a seed bead. Take the thread back through the pearls and stitch it into the doily.

DIFFERENT LENGTHS
The centre drop has one more small silver pearl than the drops on each side.

paper

equipment

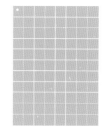

It's a part of everyday life, but take another look at paper; it can so easily be made into something beautiful. FOLDED, CUT OUT, PRINTED ON OR COMPILED into a scrapbook, paper has personality far beyond two dimensions. THE JAPANESE HAVE FOR CENTURIES TRANSFORMED SIMPLE SHEETS INTO ORIGAMI FIGURES, including the well-known origami crane. Generations of children have made pretty lanterns and paper chains at Christmas. And since the 19th century, people have been sending each other their best wishes on greeting cards. IT IS EASY TO FALL IN LOVE WITH PAPER AND ITS MANY ENTRANCING PATTERNS AND TEXTURES, and buying a single sheet will not break the bank. It may, however, inspire you to turn it into something amazing.

STEEL RULER

A steel ruler is a wonderful tool for measuring, marking and cutting a straight line. The measures on the ruler are precisely marked right from the end. The first few centimetres are also marked in half-millimetres. Unlike a timber or plastic ruler, a steel ruler's edge doesn't degrade with use. If you are using the ruler for cutting, hold it down firmly with one hand and place the craft knife or scalpel against its edge. Don't hold the craft knife too upright, as you want to use more than its tip for cutting; instead, hold it at a shallow angle to the paper.

CUTTING MAT

A self-healing cutting mat stays smooth even after repeated use and is the perfect surface for cutting. The mat is a little grippy and its surface helps keep a piece of paper in place as you cut. Some cutting mats have a measurement grid marked on them, which is useful for rough measurements and for locating the centre of shapes marked on semi-transparent paper. You'll find cutting mats in a range of sizes at craft and art suppliers, but an A3-sized mat is the most useful.

HOBBY OR PAPER KNIFE

The key to cutting paper and card is having a sharp blade firmly attached to a handle that you can easily hold at a good cutting angle (less than 35°). The paper projects in this book were done using a large (18mm) and a small (9mm) snap-blade paper/utility knife. The large knife is good for longer, straighter cuts on card; the small knife allows for finer detail. Hold the knife with your index finger resting above where the blade protrudes and your other fingers on each side. The widely available hobby knife has a variety of blades, but is designed for general hobby use (eg model making). You are best using a No. 3 or a No. 12 blade (or a No. 19, No. 20 or No. 23 blade with a larger knife); the common No. 11 blade is too pointed. A disposable scalpel may have a sharp blade, but its shape was not designed for the precision cutting of paper.

SCISSORS

There is a whole world of cutting beyond the blunt-ended "paper scissors" given to schoolchildren. The best scissors for paper craft have long, fine blades and a pointed tip for accurate cutting. Craft shears have a longer blade and are very good for making long straight cuts. Pointed trimmers have a very pointed tip that allows you to snip into awkward spots. Paper-edger scissors have a pattern on the blade so you can cut a decorative edge, such as a scallop. If after a while you find a sticky residue has built up on any of your scissors from cutting through tape and glued paper, give the blades a clean with lighter fluid or eucalyptus oil in a well-ventilated spot.

GLUE

Acid-free glue is the best choice for paper projects, as it won't discolour over time. This is particularly an issue if you are sticking photos, so choose an adhesive that is labelled "photo safe".
An all-purpose craft glue is indispensable. It dries clear and may be used full-strength or watered down and brushed on. A glue stick is also handy for sticking paper. 2-Way Glue, which comes in a squeezy pen, may be used as normal glue or be left to dry on a surface to work as a repositionable adhesive. If you are sticking thin materials or a large area, use a spray adhesive to get an even coverage (keep it out of reach of children). And remember, although these glues dry clear, any excess will show up as a shiny mark on matt paper.

TAPE

Double-sided tape, glue tape and even everyday sticky tape have a place in paper craft. There is also repositionable tape that holds items in place temporarily. Double-sided tape is brilliant for sticking two pieces of paper together without adding thickness. Double-sided adhesive dots may also be used. Glue tape does a similar job to double-sided tape, but comes in a special applicator that allows you to place the adhesive tape exactly where you want it. As with glues, choose adhesive tape that is acid-free.

STAMP & INK PAD

Having a few rubber stamps, a dye pad and acid-free coloured inks expands your design options when you're making cards or a scrapbook. A medium to large background stamp that adds a subtle all-over pattern, a pretty floral or leaf stamp and a set of alphabet letters will make a handy pack. Do your stamping on a stable, hard surface. Always clean the stamp between colours and when you finish using it; a special stamp cleaning solution includes conditioners for the rubber. Use a soft toothbrush or scrubber pad to remove the ink rather than immersing the stamp in water, as this may loosen the adhesive holding it to its backing block. Blot the stamp dry on paper towel.

handmade cards & envelopes

A card you have fashioned yourself means so much more than a store-bought item. Make a matching envelope, too.

Materials

coloured cardstock or ready-made cards (cards can be purchased ready-made in a variety of sizes or constructed very easily from cardstock or thin cardboard)

various papers, plain and printed (from specialist paper shops and scrapbooking suppliers)

scissors or paper trimmer

spray adhesive

glue pen

vellum adhesive (very good for attaching ribbons, light paper and vellum)

ribbons

buttons

paper or woven braid

double-sided tape

split-pin paper fasteners

sharp craft knife or scalpel

fine cord or thread

decorative-edged scissors

daisy wheels card

Copying the template on page 176, trace and cut three paper flowers and three contrast 35mm centres. Use split-pin paper fasteners to fix the flowers to an 8 x 23cm single-fold card.

envelope with daisy

This is to fit an 8 x 23cm vertical card.

Trace the template on page 183 onto cardstock. Cut out and score along the fold lines. Using tacky craft glue or a glue pen, glue underlap beneath opposite side at centre back. Glue up bottom flap. From contrast prints, cut a daisy outline (template on page 176) and a 35mm centre. Secure flower to the back flap with a split-pin paper fastener. Use repositionable adhesive to create a sticky back to the lower half of the flower – the envelope can then be opened and resealed a number of times.

card with mother-of-pearl buttons

Using an old paint colour chart, cut eight 27 x 35mm paint chips in graded neutral tones. Glue these neatly to a 21 x 7.5cm single-fold card, making the spaces between them even. Very lightly rule a grid through the centres of the rectangles with pencil, then use a lengthened stitch on your sewing machine to stitch carefully over the grid. Knot the threads neatly on the back. Stitch a mother-of-pearl button to the centre of each grid.

stitched envelope

This is to fit a 21 x 7.5cm card.

Trace the template on page 179 onto medium-weight cream paper. Cut out, then score along the fold lines. Lightly rule the front of the envelope and the upper flap into a grid.

Use a lengthened stitch on your sewing machine to stitch carefully over the grid, starting and stopping exactly at the fold lines. Knot the threads neatly on the back.

Before gluing the envelope, stitch a mother-of-pearl button to the centre of the back flap, as marked, and another on one back section, close to the centre back line, as marked. Carefully glue the centre back edges, then the bottom flap (the buttons should line up with each other). To close the envelope, use a little matching thread to wind around the buttons in a figure-of-eight.

ENVELOPE WITH DAISY
Secure the daisy flower to the back flap of the envelope with a split-pin fastener. If you put repositionable adhesive on the bottom half of the flower's back, the envelope can be opened and resealed.

STITCHED ENVELOPE
This envelope has a grid of stitching on one side, and two small mother-of-pearl buttons on the back. Thread wound around these buttons holds the envelope closed.

WINDMILL CARD
To make the windmill, cut two-thirds of the way down the diagonals you have drawn on the paper, then fold in the corners and hold in place with a split-pin fastener.

windmill card

To make the windmill, start with a 12cm square of double-sided paper. (Double-sided paper is available from scrapbooking suppliers. If you can't find it, use spray adhesive to glue two sheets together.) Lightly rule two intersecting diagonal lines across the centre of the square, from corner to corner. Cut two-thirds of the way down each diagonal, then fold the corners, one after another, into the centre and secure with a split-pin paper fastener. Glue two 1.5cm paper strips vertically and horizontally onto an 11 x 15cm single-fold card, then use double-sided tape to fix the windmill to the intersection of the paper strips.

card with braid and window

Start with a 10 x 16.5cm single-fold card. Using a scalpel or sharp craft knife, cut a 3.5 x 13.5cm window from the front of the card, positioning the window 1.5cm in from the edges. From a contrast striped paper, cut a 10 x 16.5cm rectangle and, using spray adhesive, glue the paper to the inside front of the card, so that it shows in the window. Glue a strip of paper braid into the window. (This pink paper braid came from Pulp; www.pulpcreativepaper.com.au.)

striped envelope

This is to fit a 10 x 16.5cm card.
Trace the template on page 182 onto the wrong side of the striped paper. Cut out and score along the fold lines. Using tacky craft glue or a glue pen, stick the side flaps beneath the back section.
Glue a motif or sticker to the centre back edge of the flap – you can use repositionable glue to make it resealable.

card with large centre button

Rule and score a 15 x 22cm rectangle of cream cardstock so that the edges meet at the centre front, creating an 11 x 15cm card. Cut two rectangles of a co-ordinating cream print paper, each 4.5 x 14cm, and stick them to each front flap. Stitch an antique button to the centre front edge of one flap and, to the opposite flap, attach a narrow cord which can be wound around the button to close the card.

CARD WITH WINDOW
A simple but effective idea, this card has striped paper glued to its inside. A window is cut in the cover, then a line of braid is positioned beneath it.

STRIPED ENVELOPE
When you trace the envelope template on the striped paper, make sure that its edges are in line with the stripes. Repositionable glue on the back of the flower makes it resealable.

PHOTO-FRAME CARD
The size and position of the window in this card will depend on the photo being displayed. You may mount the photo using simple diagonal slits or photo corners.

photo-frame card

Cut a 5cm window in the front of a 15 x 10.5cm single-fold card – the fold can be on the long or short edge. (The actual size and position of the window will depend on the subject of your photograph – the window should provide a "teaser" to the larger photo inside the card.) Use a striped grosgrain ribbon to "frame" the window, cutting the corners into accurate mitres. Using double-sided tape to fix the ribbon will help stop the edges fraying. Fix the photo on the inside back of the card, using photo corners or simply cut diagonal slits in the card. (Striped grosgrain ribbon is available from Speckle Farm, www.specklefarm.com.au.)

origami crane card

Start with an 11cm square single-fold card. Cut an 8cm square and a 6cm square from different coloured papers and fix to the centre of the card. Finish with a small paper crane, folded from co-ordinating origami paper (see folding instructions on page 92).

embossed hearts card

From nine co-ordinating solid coloured papers (or an old paint colour chart), cut nine 3cm squares. Emboss each square with a tiny heart. To do this, you can buy embossing kits from scrapbooking suppliers, or use an embossing tool (or even the end of a steel knitting needle) with a small heart stencil. Position the stencil on top of the coloured square and, working on the wrong side, press around the outline of the stencil with the embossing tool to make the pattern stand out on the right side. Glue the finished squares to an 11cm square single-fold card.

square envelope with curved flaps

This is to fit an 11cm square card.
Trace the template on page 181 onto single- or double-sided paper. Cut out around the curved edges, score along the outline of the square and fold in the flaps, one after another in a clockwise direction, so that they interlock. Place a small sticker over the centre point to seal, if desired. You can also fold the flaps of this envelope, sides first, then bottom and top, and seal with a sticker or sealing wax for a different look.

EMBOSSING KIT
You may use an embossing kit such as this to emboss shapes, or trace around the edge of a stencil with a knitting needle.

SQUARE ENVELOPE
The curved flaps make this very simple envelope look special. Simply cut out around the curves, score the inner folds, and fold in the flaps.

Simply cut a piece of vellum
or paper to the size of a ready-
made envelope, slip it inside
and glue in place.

CHRISTMAS TREE CARD
Ribbon is threaded through
the slits on the triangle
to make the Christmas tree
shape on the right side.
Secure the ribbon ends
with sticky tape.

vellum card

Cut an 8 x 12.5cm rectangle of printed paper vellum and use a very
light coat of vellum adhesive to stick this to a 15 x 10.5cm single-fold
cream card. Fix at the corners with silver split-pin fasteners.

envelope with vellum lining

This method can be adjusted to fit any size of commercial envelope.
Cut a sheet of vellum (or other paper) to the width of your envelope.
Slip it inside the envelope and lightly trace around the upper flap
edge, below the gummed section. Cut out around the traced line,
then score along the flap crease. Glue in place only along the flap
edge, using glue sparingly to avoid show-through. (If you plan to
make a number of these using vellum, you can get special vellum
adhesive from scrapbooking suppliers.)

circles card

Cut nine 35mm circles from different coloured papers and, using
a light coat of spray adhesive or vellum adhesive, position circles
on a 14cm square single-fold card. Very lightly rule a grid through
the centre of the circles with pencil, then use a lengthened stitch
on your sewing machine to stitch carefully over the grid. Knot the
threads neatly on the back.

Christmas tree card

In the centre of the inside front flap of a 15 x 10.5cm single-fold card,
lightly rule a triangle, 8.5cm high and 6cm wide at the base.
Using a scalpel, cut slits along the side edges of the triangle: cut the
first ones 2cm long from the bottom corners; leave 1cm and cut the
next slits 1.5cm long on each side; leave 1cm and cut the third slits
2cm long on each side; leave 1cm and cut out the remaining tip of
the triangle. Thread ribbon of the appropriate width through the slits
and across the front of the card, fixing the ends on the inside with
sticky tape. (We used a combination of satin, organza and metallic
ribbon.) At the top, simply stick the ribbon behind the exposed
triangle. Approximately 1cm below the bottom edge of the triangle,
rule a wedge shape, 3cm across the top, 2cm across the bottom and
1.5cm high. Slit the edges and thread with gold ribbon, as before.
Glue a sequin star to the top of the tree to complete.

TASSEL ENVELOPE
A loop attached to the tassel can be stretched between the two split-pin fasteners, holding this envelope closed.

fabric-printed square card

Using spray adhesive, glue a 9cm square of fabric-printed paper (from scrapbooking suppliers) to an 11cm square single-fold card. If you want to use real fabric, press iron-on interfacing onto the back of the fabric before cutting, to prevent fraying.

tassel envelope

This is to fit an 11cm square card.

Trace the template on page 180 onto the wrong side of a square of scrapbook paper. Cut out and score along the fold lines. Using tacky craft glue or a glue pen, stick the side flaps beneath the back. Attach two split-pin paper fasteners – one in the centre of the lower edge of the flap and one in the centre of the back, about 1.5cm below the first. Purchase a small tassel and attach a small loop to the top so that the two fastener pins can be looped together, holding the envelope closed.

cut-out flower card

It is important to start with cardstock for this card, rather than a ready-made card, as you don't want a scoreline across the centre of the flower. Start with a 14 x 20cm rectangle of cardstock, and the same size rectangle of contrast paper. Using spray adhesive, glue the paper rectangle to the cardstock.

Lightly rule a line across the halfway point of the card on the print side (finished card will be 14 x 10cm). Trace the flower outline (see page 176) onto thin cardboard and cut out for a template.

Lining up the dotted line of the flower with the halfway line on the card, trace half a flower into the centre on the print side of the card and carefully cut along the traced lines with a scalpel.

Score the fold line on each side of the flower (do not score across the centre of the flower) and fold the card gently in half to release the cut section of the flower. Trim the lower front edge of the card using paper scissors with a decorative edge, such as a scallop, to show the printed paper underneath.

CUT-OUT FLOWER CARD
Score the fold line on each side of the flower shape, but not across its centre. The flower shape is released when the card is folded.

graphic squares card

Start with an 11cm square single-fold card. From a range of solid coloured papers or Canson paper, cut four squares: 3cm, 5cm, 7cm and 9cm. Glue each of the squares to the centre of the next larger square, then glue the largest paper square to the centre of the card.

paper boxes

These little origami boxes can hold small gifts. If you use stripes, have them on the diagonal, so when the box is folded they are straight. Heavier paper is better for the larger sizes.

Materials

paper (90gsm to 160gsm)
paper knife or sharp paper scissors
pencil
ruler
bone scorer or paper scissors
glue stick

Method

1. Cut squares of paper for the lid and base (see Box Sizes).
2. On the wrong side of the paper, lightly mark the squares' diagonals. This will be a guide for the initial folds.
3. Fold corners of each square into centre, using pencil marks as a guide. Use a scorer or the blunt side of scissor blades to make creases sharp.
4. On the square for the base, fold two opposite sides to meet at the centre, crease and unfold. Repeat for the other two sides.
5. Accuracy is needed to make a snug-fitting lid. Use the measures given in Box Sizes as an initial guide, but to ensure a good fit, measure the distance between the side folds on the square for the base; on the square for the lid, fold in the opposite sides so the distance between the two folds is 2mm wider than what you measured on the base. Crease and unfold. Repeat on remaining sides.
6. At each corner of the paper, on both the base and the lid, there will be a square formed by previous folds. Fold a diagonal crease across this square with the point coming inwards. Repeat on all corners.
7. For both the base and the lid, unfold two opposite sides. Refold the other sides along the creases so they stand upright. Fold up a third side, tucking the small corner creases under the flap. Repeat on the remaining side. Glue points in the centre.

FOLD IN THE SIDES
For a snug-fitting lid, the distance between the side folds on the lid should be 2mm more than between the side folds on the base. Use a bone scorer or a pair of scissors to get sharp creases.

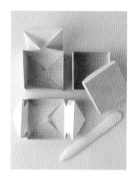

ASSEMBLING THE SIDES
Fold in two opposite sides so they stand upright. Fold up a third side, tucking the corner creases under its flap. Fold the final side and glue down the ends of the paper neatly.

BOX SIZES

Box	Square for base	Fold for base sides	Square for lid	Fold for lid sides
5cm	14cm	2.5cm	10cm	1cm
7cm*	20cm	3.5cm	14.5cm	1.5cm
10cm**	28cm	5cm	20cm	1.9cm

* Largest size possible from an A4 sheet.

** Largest size possible from an A3 sheet.

To make boxes of other sizes, remember that the paper for the lid measures 72% of the paper for the base. The fold for the lid side is 10% of the length of the lid paper. (Follow instructions in Step 5 for an exact fit.) The final box you make is about 35% the size of the paper used for its base.

decorative lanterns

Delicate paper decorations look wonderful strung across
a window or hung on a Christmas tree.

Materials

paper in three different colours or patterns
pencil
ruler
cutting board
paper knife
decorative hole punches, optional
glue tape roller
double-sided tape
sticky tape (16mm wide)
23cm lengths of fine wire, to make handles

Method

1. To make the inside cylinder, cut out a rectangle 100mm x 160mm. Mark a vertical line 15mm from one end of the 160mm length – this will be the overlap when the cylinder is joined.

2. Cut a 130mm x 165mm rectangle from each of the other papers.

3. On the back of the larger rectangles, rule horizontal lines 20mm in from the top and bottom edges. Between these two lines, mark and cut a series of vertical lines 15mm apart (see photo).

4. Secure the inside cylinder with glue tape (double width), matching the overlap line with the other short edge.

5. Place remaining rectangles pattern side up. On one only, attach glue tape to the wrong side, along half the length of the top and bottom edges. Attach it to the other rectangle, positioning it 2mm in from the top and bottom edges, and halfway along (see photo).

6. Flip joined rectangles over and apply double-sided tape or glue tape to the exposed halves of the outer sheet (see photo). Double-sided tape is best for the short edge of the inner sheet (see photo).

7. So they fit snugly, roll the rectangles around the cylinder. Join the two slit sheets, maintaining the 2mm gap between the top and bottom edges, and join each sheet to its other end.

8. Slide the inside cylinder into the now rolled outer layers. Take three short pieces of sticky tape and attach the cylinder so it's about half the width of the sticky tape (8mm) short of the end of the outer sheets. Repeat for the other end of the cylinder.

9. Bend wire for handle over a glass to get a good curve. Make two small holes in the top of the cylinder and thread the wire through.

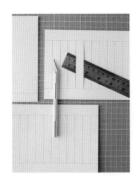

MAKING THE SLITS
Mark and cut a series of vertical lines between the two 20mm marks on the larger rectangles. If you are cutting decorative shapes in the paper with a hole punch, do it at this stage.

JOINING OUTSIDE SHEETS
Attach one rectangle to the other, halfway along its length and 2mm in from the top and bottom edges. This makes the outside sheet bulge out a little more than the inside one.

ADDING THE TAPE
Put glue tape or double-sided tape on the inside edges of the rectangles as shown. Standard double-sided tape is twice the width of glue tape; cut it in half lengthways before using it on the top and bottom edges of the rectangles.

MAKING IT FIT
Roll the outside rectangles around the cylinder to work out exactly where they should join. This will ensure a good fit. Join the rectangles with the double-sided tape or glue tape that is already in place.

INSERT THE CYLINDER
Slide the cylinder into the centre of the now rolled outer layers. Attach it 8mm short of the top and bottom edges of the outside papers.

holiday scrapbook

Memories of a holiday become extra special when they're gathered in a scrapbook. Turn it into a work of art.

Ethan at the beach

Materials

two-page co-ordinating layout (we used Kolette Layered Paper Flip Pack "Mustard")
turquoise blue rickrack braid
scrapbooking glue
black and white photographs (enlarge and crop some of your images so that you have a variety of close-ups and landscape shots)
vellum stickers: "Bubbles", "Seashells"
sheet of fine sandpaper
turquoise blue paper
small sharp scissors

Method

1. If you are not using a ready-made co-ordinating layout, you will need to construct two pages from a series of yellow papers. Stitch on cotton tape and rows of machine stitching for interest, using the photograph as a guide.
2. Glue a line of rickrack braid to each page.
3. Sketch child's name in simple childish letters on the back of a sheet of fine sandpaper (remember to write back to front!). Cut out the letters and glue them to a sheet of turquoise paper. Cut out again, leaving a 2mm border of blue around the sand letters, creating a "shadow".
4. Using the photograph as a guide, position photographs, stickers and cut-out letters on the pages until you are happy with the layout, then fix or glue each item in place.

Phoebe at the beach

Materials

two-page co-ordinating layout (we used Kolette Layered Paper Flip Pack "Blueberry")
white acrylic paint
paintbrush
yellow stripe scrapbooking paper
black and white photographs (crop some of your images so that you have a variety of close-ups and landscape shots)
vellum stickers: "Bubbles", "Seashells"
sheet of fine sandpaper
small sharp scissors
scrapbooking glue

Method

1. If you are not using a ready-made co-ordinating layout, you will need to construct two pages from a series of blue papers. Use torn edges and stitch on cotton tape for interest, using the photograph on page 84 as a guide.
2. Using a little white acrylic paint and a dry paintbrush, brush the edges of the torn papers with white to look like sea foam.
3. Cut rectangles of yellow stripe paper larger than your photograph. Roughly cut out the vellum stickers and letters of the child's name.
4. Draw tiny footprints on the back of fine sandpaper and cut out with small sharp scissors.
5. Position papers, photographs, stickers, letters and footprints on the pages, then fix or glue each item in place. See photo on page 84 at bottom right.

scrapbook cover

Materials

purchased scrapbook (preferably with a plain paper or vinyl cover)

0.5 metres thin, strong fabric (we used seeded calico – excessively thick or textured fabric can be too bulky)

spray adhesive

tacky craft glue

scalpel or small, sharp scissors

sheets of thin cardboard, for endpapers

small photographs (we printed our photographs in cyan on the computer, for a blue look)

rub-on letters (we used Phrase Café "Christopher")

scrapbooking glue

Method

1. Take scrapbook apart by removing the adjustable screws. Set pages aside and reserve the front and back covers and the spine cover. For each cover, cut a piece of fabric to fit (including the folded flap), plus 5–10cm extra for turning around all edges.

2. For the spine cover, cut a piece the same size, plus 2cm extra all round.

3. Lay one cover, with the flap fully extended, right side up, on some sheets of newspaper and spray evenly with spray adhesive. Place the cover, sticky side down, in the centre of the wrong side of one fabric piece. Check to see that there are no wrinkles and that you are allowing for the flap to be folded back to the inside. As though you were covering a book with paper, fold the excess fabric to the inside (you may need to trim it a little if you have too much, especially on the flap), and secure in place with tacky craft glue, folding the corners into neat creases. Repeat this process for the remaining cover.

4. Apply the same process to the spine cover.

5. To neaten the inside of the covers (and the spine cover, if you like, though this isn't strictly necessary), cut thin cardboard to fit the inside of the covers (with flaps extended). Cut it a few millimetres smaller all round than the cover itself. Spray with spray adhesive and fix in place, again taking care that the flap will still fold. Using a scalpel or small, sharp scissors, cut away the fabric and paper from the holes for the screws in all sections.

6. Reassemble album.

7. Glue small photographs to the outside in a neat row and use rub-on letters (they can be rubbed directly onto the fabric) to label your album.

JOURNALLING

Write captions in the scrapbook to tell the story behind the images. Record the names of the people in the photos, where and when the events took place, and also why people were there – the details that might otherwise be forgotten. Use a pen with acid-free ink so that it won't affect the paper over time.

Having a torn edge on paper gives a softer effect. To tear in a straight line, first crease the paper, then dampen the crease with a wet paintbrush before tearing. For a freeform effect, tear dry paper.

Remember that you have to write back to front when you sketch the letters on the back of the sandpaper.

Glue the letters on turquoise paper and cut around them to make a 2mm shadow effect.

Fold the fabric to the inside of the cover as if you were covering a book with paper. Trim off any excess fabric, then hold in place with craft glue.

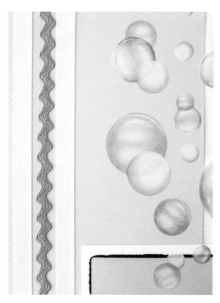

Lines of braid add texture, and you can also hand- or machine-stitch the paper. Use a slightly longer stitch on your sewing machine, and for hand sewing, mark and pierce stitching holes before you start.

The "Phoebe at the beach" layout includes little "sand" footprints, stickers, and torn paper edges brushed with white paint to look like sea foam.

doily fairy lights

Dress up a special occasion with a string of fairy lights trimmed with delicate paper doily shades.

Materials

string of fairy lights (the one shown
  has 20 bulbs)
165mm diameter paper doilies, enough
  to cover the lights
2 sheets acetate suitable for use with an
  overhead projector
protractor
pencil
sharp paper knife or sharp paper scissors
cutting board
double-sided tape

Method

1. Mark the centre of the doily. Using the protractor measure and mark (using the centre as the origin point) an angle of 135°.
2. Cut and remove the marked wedge from the doily. If using a paper knife it must be sharp and the blade held at a shallow angle to the cutting board to prevent it tearing the doily as you cut.
3. Cut a tiny circle in the doily's centre; this will accommodate the light's wiring. Different light strings have different cord arrangements and within one string some bulbs may have more cords than others. Start by removing just a few millimetres then test by temporarily forming the shade (see below). Adjust the size and shape of the hole to fit cables. Later shades (for the same cable arrangement) can be made using the first shade as a template.
4. Cut acetate with knife as per template (see page 177). Slight changes may need to be made to the centre hole to accommodate the fairy lights' wires.
5. Put acetate around the base of the bulb fitting and fasten by sliding the tab through the slot. Form doily shade around acetate with an overlap on the join of about 15mm at the outer edge of the doily, reducing to just a couple of millimetres at the centre. Fix join using pieces of double-sided tape.

ADJUST CENTRE HOLES
You may need to slightly adjust the centre holes to accommodate the wiring on the lights. Use sharp paper scissors or a paper knife to carefully trim the hole.

WRAPPING AROUND
The doily will overlap by about 15mm on its outer edge, but only a few millimetres in the centre. This gives a sweet tulip shape to the shade.

WARNING
Do not switch on the lights and leave them unattended.

silhouettes

Turn your family photos into a collection of classic silhouettes, presented in matching frames. All it takes is a photocopier and a steady hand for cutting.

Materials

set of matching frames
selection of photos
card weight white paper
card weight coloured papers
paper knife or hobby knife
cutting mat
paper glue or clear-drying PVA
paintbrush to apply glue

Method

1. Decide the size of the silhouette you want to make. This will depend on the frame in which it's to be displayed.
2. Photocopy your chosen photo, adjusting the print-out on the photocopier until it's the appropriate size. You can also do this by scanning the image on a computer and adjusting the size. You may have to cut the card to size to fit in the photocopier or printer. (A4 size is 210mm x 297mm.)
3. Cut out the image with a sharp paper knife or hobby knife. The printed side will be the back, so the final silhouette will be the reverse of this printed image.
4. Cut coloured card to fit in the frames. Using paper glue, or watered-down PVA, paint the back of the silhouette shapes with glue and position on the coloured card, sliding it into its final position. Carefully clean up any excess glue with a damp cloth.
5. Mount in the frame.

COPY THE IMAGE
Either photocopy or print out the image. Adjusting the contrast settings on the photocopier may give you a better defined edge. Remember that the reverse side will be shown in the final silhouette.

CUTTING OUT
Carefully cut around the silhouette. Use a sharp blade and don't be in a rush. One slip of the hand and you will have to start over.

NOTE The best photos to make into silhouettes are of individuals on their own, with little happening in the background. Do a quick check by squinting at the photo so you reduce the image to its basic shape.

origami crane mobile

Japanese tradition holds that if you make a thousand paper cranes your wish will be granted. This delicate mobile has fewer cranes, but it brings happiness just the same.

Materials

18 pieces origami paper, 15cm square (you may have more or fewer cranes; see next page for folding instructions)

200mm diameter galvanised ring (available from craft stores)

25mm diameter washer (optional)

1.4 metres silk ribbon (to cover ring)

craft glue (any PVA adhesive that dries clear may be used)

beading needle

9 metres fine white beading thread

36 small pearl beads (3mm diameter)

72 clear seed beads

ruler

marker pen

1.6 metres double-sided satin ribbon, 4mm wide

Method

To assemble the mobile

1. Wind the silk ribbon around the galvanised ring. Dab a little glue on the ribbon's end to secure it; let dry. Do the same to the washer.

2. Draw the beading thread through the leader loop on the needle (see page 188), then thread on one seed bead and one pearl bead. Push needle through the centre point of the back of a crane and out the hole at the crane's "belly". Thread on another pearl bead, then knot the thread around the bead. Use two overhand knots, then three half-hitch knots to hold it in place (see page 188).

3. Pull up the thread so the bottom bead nestles into the crane's belly. Using a ruler, measure and mark the thread 5cm above the crane. Make another mark to show the final length of the drop (see Measures below). Add 5cm to this (to allow for tying) and cut the thread.

4. Tie a double knot at the first 5cm mark above the crane. Rethread needle, then thread on three seed beads, and tie a double knot just above the beads. Repeat for other cranes.

5. Take one of the cranes on the 47cm (+5cm) lengths of thread. Make a loop at the marked length and place over the pearl bead at the base of one of the first nine cranes (on the graduated lengths). Pull thread tight and tie in place. Repeat, so that each crane on a 47cm length is below a crane on a graduated length. Tie the first nine cranes around the galvanised ring, shortest to longest. Trim ends.

6. To make a hanging loop, take two 80cm lengths of satin ribbon and lay in a cross over the ring. Pass 3cm of each end under the ring and loop to the back of the satin ribbon. Secure with craft glue, let dry, then stitch in place. Pull the ribbon loops through the washer to form a loop at the top for hanging.

THREADING THROUGH
Push the needle through the exact centre point on the back of the crane, where the two diagonal folds intersect.

POSITIONING THE KNOTS
You may use a pair of tapered tweezers or a toothpick to position the knots in place. Place it in the loop of the knot and move it down the thread to where the knot should be.

MEASURES Instructions are for nine cranes on drops of 18cm 23cm 28cm 33cm 38cm 43cm 48cm 53cm 58cm. Nine more cranes are on drops of 47cm.

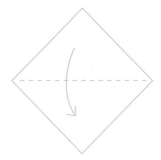

Fold the square of origami paper in half diagonally with the patterned/coloured side out. Fold the resulting triangle in half again, then unfold.

Pull up the top left-hand corner. Pull out the sides of the paper layers. Carefully press the point down flat on top of the triangle's apex.

Fold the sides out to form a small square (Squash Fold). Flip over and repeat on the other side.

Throughout the rest of the construction keep the corner of the square joining the closed folded edges to the top.

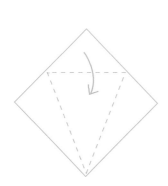

Fold the lower left and right edges of the top layer to the centre line. Fold the top point across the line formed where the side points now meet.

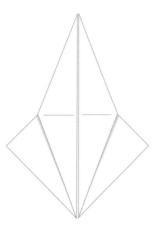

Unfold the three folds you just made, then lift the bottom point of the top sheet up and over the top point. Fold the edges lifted by this process in to the centre line, creating a narrow diamond shape (Petal Fold).

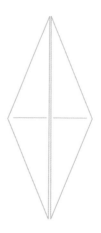

Flip over and repeat the Petal Fold on the other side to complete the diamond-shaped Bird Base.

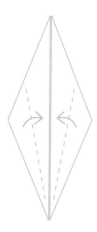

Fold the lower left and right sides in to the centre line. Flip.

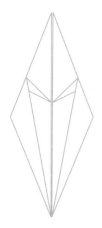

Fold in the lower left and right sides on the other side to create a kite shape.

Open out the left side and fold up the bottom point to start making a three-pointed crown shape. Close up the side to create an inside reverse fold, making sure the edges of the folded-up section are in line with the outside. Repeat on the right side to finish the crown shape.

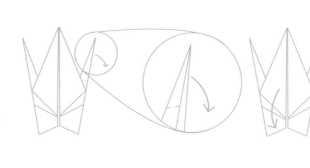

Take one of the side points and fold it down at 45° to make the beak.

Gently pull the wings outwards to expand the body section.

Fold

Open out layers

Crease for the fold

cooking

equipment

Sharing food is part of friendship, and the simple acts of cooking and giving make a deep impression on those who receive your present. You may PREPARE A JAR OF PRESERVES THAT WILL KEEP FOR MONTHS IN THE KITCHEN CUPBOARD, or a package of sweet morsels to be popped in the mouth immediately – all will be appreciated. The presentation can make the gift even more memorable. MAKE PRETTY BOXES AND SEARCH OUT COLOURFUL RIBBONS OR BRIGHT PATTY-CAKE PAPERS to package up your goods, and choose them in tones that play off the colours of the food. The small extra effort involved is another way of showing you care. There is a belief that THE GOOD THOUGHTS OF THE MAKER TRANSFER TO THE FOOD, so when you're cooking, do it with love.

OVEN TRAYS

Oven tray or baking sheet is a generic term for a broad, flat baking tray. Biscuit/slice trays and lamington trays have deeper sides than biscuit or scone trays, but all may be used to bake biscuits or cookies – what's important is that the trays heat evenly. Like other bakeware, these trays may come with a standard or a non-stick finish.

CAKE TINS

Most cake tins are made of metal and most types are available with a non-stick surface (though it's still a good idea to oil or grease the non-stick ones for baking). There is also more expensive silicone bakeware, which is permanently non-stick and easily releases cakes and muffins. It may also be used in a microwave oven. Cake tins and muffin trays come in different sizes and it's important to use the size specified in a recipe. Having a smaller or larger tin affects the cooking time. Even if a mixture is to be cooled and set, rather than cooked, it's best to use the same size of container as in the recipe, so you achieve a similar looking result.

BAKING PAPER

Baking paper has a non-stick coating and may be used instead of oil to stop items sticking to bakeware. If the baking paper is to cover the side of a baking tin, spraying a little cooking oil on the surface first makes it easier to keep the paper in place. The paper is also useful when you're storing or packaging items; placing a piece between layers of brownies or cakes stops them sticking to each other.

CAKE COOLING RACK

A cake rack is incredibly useful for cooling cakes and biscuits. You could also use one as a place to rest a hot saucepan. The rack has feet so air can circulate underneath, and it may be made of stainless steel, chrome-covered steel or have a non-stick surface. Look for one that has its metal bars laid out in a grid, as this gives better support for items. Racks that have one set of bars running lengthways are more properly used as roasting racks.

COOKIE CUTTERS

Using cookie cutters is a quick and easy way to make pretty-looking biscuits – and they'll all be the right size. Traditional shapes such as gingerbread men, stars and hearts have a timeless appeal, and their outlines may be accentuated with a little icing. There are cookie cutters especially for Christmas, ones shaped like animals, birds, leaves... the variety is almost endless. Even plain circle cutters are useful to have around.

MIXING BOWLS AND MEASURES

When it comes to mixing bowls, size matters. Bowls of a particular size are suited to different tasks. Small bowls are best for beating eggs; a medium bowl is good for blending dry ingredients and a large bowl may be used for mixing batters. Traditional ceramic bowls look beautiful, but a set of inexpensive stainless-steel bowls in different sizes will work just as well – just don't put them in the microwave. Measuring cups are another essential for cooking; made in plastic or metal, they usually come in a set of four, with 1-cup, ½-cup, ⅓-cup and ¼-cup sizes.

MIXER

Whisking egg whites and mixing cake batters is a much simpler job when you have an electric mixer. Inexpensive, hand-held mixers are adequate for preparing most cake batters, but committed cooks may prefer a more heavy-duty benchtop mixer that can also handle bread dough and biscuit mixtures. Although it will work very well, a benchtop mixer can be pricey; decide how much you'd really use it before you invest in one. Some food processors also have settings for beating egg whites, mixing cake batters or making pastry.

preserved lemons

The exotic flavours of the Middle East include home-preserved lemons. They are easy to make and, packed in a pretty jar, will be greatly appreciated as a gift.

Ingredients

10 medium lemons (1.4kg), quartered
1 cup (250g) salt
1 bay leaf, torn
1 cinnamon stick, quartered
1 teaspoon coriander seeds, lightly bruised
    to release their fragrance
2 cups (500ml) lemon juice

PREPARATION TIME 10 minutes
MAKES two 750ml jars

Method

1. Combine lemons and salt in large bowl.
2. Pack lemon mixture, bay leaf, cinnamon and seeds firmly into two 3-cup (750ml) sterilised jars. Pour over enough juice to cover lemons completely; seal jars tightly. Stand in a cool, dry place for at least 1 month.
3. To serve, remove and discard the pulp from the rind. Rinse rind well and slice thinly. It may be served as part of a platter with olives and cubed fetta cheese, and sprinkled with olive oil. The rind may also be used to flavour tagines, casseroles, fish and salads.

To sterilise jars: Place clean jars on their sides in a large saucepan or boiler. Cover completely with cold water. Place lid on pan and bring water to the boil. Boil, covered, for 20 minutes. Carefully remove the jars from the water with a pair of tongs. Let them drain, then stand right-way up on a wooden board.

You may either cut through the lemons completely, or cut down to just above the stem end and place salt within the slits.

GREMOLATA WITH PRESERVED LEMON

Crush 2 cloves of garlic and combine with 1½ tablespoons chopped preserved lemon rind, ½ cup chopped flat-leaf parsley and 2 tablespoons of olive oil. Sprinkle the gremolata over cooked meats, poultry or fish.

chocolate truffles

A delightful selection of chocolate truffles you made yourself will long be remembered. Present them with a flourish.

peanut butter and milk chocolate truffles

Ingredients

⅓ cup (80ml) thickened cream

200g milk eating chocolate, chopped coarsely

¼ cup (70g) unsalted crunchy peanut butter

¾ cup (110g) crushed peanuts

PREPARATION TIME 40 minutes (plus refrigeration time)
COOKING TIME 5 minutes
MAKES 30

Method

1. Place cream and chocolate in a small saucepan, stirring over low heat until smooth; stir in peanut butter. Transfer to small bowl. Cover; refrigerate 3 hours or overnight.

2. Working with a quarter of the chocolate mixture at a time (refrigerate remaining mixture until needed), roll rounded teaspoons into balls; place on ungreased oven tray. Refrigerate truffles until firm.

3. Working quickly, roll balls in peanuts, return to tray; refrigerate truffles until firm.

white choc, lemon, lime and coconut truffles

Ingredients

½ cup (125ml) coconut cream

2 teaspoons finely grated lime rind

2 teaspoons finely grated lemon rind

360g white eating chocolate, chopped coarsely

1¼ cups (85g) shredded coconut

PREPARATION TIME 40 minutes (plus refrigeration time)
COOKING TIME 5 minutes
MAKES 30

Method

1. Combine coconut cream, rinds and chocolate in a small saucepan; stir over low heat until smooth. Transfer mixture to small bowl. Cover; refrigerate 3 hours or overnight.

2. Working with a quarter of the chocolate mixture at a time (refrigerate remaining mixture until needed), roll rounded teaspoons into balls; place on ungreased oven tray. Refrigerate truffles until firm.

3. Working quickly, roll truffles in coconut, return to tray; refrigerate until firm.

dark chocolate and ginger truffles

Ingredients
⅓ cup (80ml) thickened cream
200g dark eating chocolate, chopped coarsely
½ cup (115g) glacé ginger, chopped finely
¼ cup (25g) cocoa powder

PREPARATION TIME 40 minutes (plus refrigeration time)
COOKING TIME 5 minutes
MAKES 30

Method
1. Combine cream and chocolate in a small saucepan, stirring over low heat until smooth; stir in ginger. Transfer to small bowl. Cover; refrigerate 3 hours or overnight.
2. Working with a quarter of the chocolate mixture at a time (refrigerate remaining mixture until needed), roll rounded teaspoons into balls; place on ungreased oven tray. Refrigerate truffles until firm.
3. Working quickly, roll balls in cocoa, return to tray; refrigerate truffles until firm.

craisin and port chocolate truffles

Ingredients
¼ cup (60ml) thickened cream
200g dark eating chocolate, chopped coarsely
2 tablespoons port
⅓ cup (50g) craisins, chopped coarsely
300g white eating chocolate, melted

PREPARATION TIME 40 minutes (plus refrigeration time)
COOKING TIME 5 minutes
MAKES 30

Method
1. Combine cream and chopped chocolate in a small saucepan; stir over low heat until smooth, stir in port and craisins. Transfer to small bowl, cover; refrigerate 3 hours or overnight.
2. Working with a quarter of the chocolate mixture at a time (refrigerate remaining mixture until needed), roll rounded teaspoons into balls; place on ungreased oven tray. Freeze truffles until firm.
3. Working quickly, dip truffles in melted chocolate then roll gently in hands to coat evenly, return to tray; refrigerate until firm.

coconut fortune cookies

Place a special message inside these delicate cookies,
package them in a Chinese takeaway carton and give them
to someone who needs a special treat.

Ingredients

2 egg whites
$\frac{1}{3}$ cup (55g) icing sugar mixture
1 teaspoon coconut essence
30g butter, melted
$\frac{1}{3}$ cup (50g) plain flour
$\frac{1}{4}$ cup (20g) desiccated coconut, toasted

PREPARATION TIME 40 minutes (making mix, cooking and
folding cookies)
COOKING TIME 5 minutes each tray
MAKES 45

Method

1. Prepare small slips of paper with "fortunes".
2. Preheat oven to moderate (180°C). Grease and lightly flour oven trays; mark two 8cm circles on each tray.
3. Beat egg whites in small bowl with electric mixer until just foamy, gradually beat in sifted icing sugar, essence and butter. Stir in sifted flour, mix until smooth.
4. Place a level teaspoon of mixture in the centre of each marked circle on the trays, spread evenly to cover circles completely; sprinkle evenly with a little coconut.
5. Bake, one tray at a time, in moderate oven (180°C) about 5 minutes or until lightly browned around the edges, remove from oven. Working quickly, place one prepared slip of paper on each cookie, then lift cookies from tray, fold in half, then lightly bend cookies over the rim of a glass; cool for 30 seconds. Place cookies on wire rack to cool completely. Repeat with remaining cookie mixture and coconut.

TIP

An easy way to make the "fortunes" for these cookies is to print a selection of messages onto plain vellum paper using an inkjet or laser printer. Cut the paper into strips with a paper or hobby knife.

peanut butter brownies

Rich, dark and delightful, these will appeal as much to adults as children. The taste combination of peanut butter and chocolate is an American classic.

Ingredients

180g butter, chopped
150g dark eating chocolate, chopped
1¾ cups (385g) caster sugar
4 eggs, beaten lightly
1 teaspoon vanilla essence
¾ cup (110g) plain flour
2 tablespoons self-raising flour
⅓ cup (35g) cocoa powder
50g dark eating chocolate, chopped, extra
⅓ cup (95g) crunchy peanut butter

PREPARATION TIME 20 minutes
COOKING TIME 50 minutes
MAKES 24

Method

1. Preheat oven to moderately slow (160ºC). Grease a 20cm x 30cm lamington pan; line base and two opposite sides with baking paper.
2. Melt butter and chocolate in medium saucepan, stir over low heat, without boiling, until mixture is smooth; cool until just warm.
3. Stir in sugar, egg and essence, then sifted flours, cocoa and extra chocolate.
4. Pour mixture into prepared pan. Drop small spoonfuls of peanut butter into the chocolate mixture and swirl through the mixture with a knife.
5. Bake in moderately slow oven (160ºC) about 50 minutes or until firm; cool in pan. Cut into 24 pieces.

Swirl spoonfuls of peanut butter through the brownie mixture, rather than mixing it in. This gives delicious pockets of peanut butter in the finished brownies.

TIP
A pretty way to present these brownies is to wrap individual pieces in cocktail size napkins and tie them with twine. It's a delicious little package to unwrap.

choc nut biscotti

A jar of classic Italian biscotti is a wonderful thing to receive, and these look particularly attractive. Give them to a friend along with a package of good-quality coffee beans.

Ingredients

1 cup (220g) caster sugar
2 eggs
1⅔ cups (250g) plain flour
1 teaspoon baking powder
1 cup (150g) shelled pistachios, roasted
½ cup (70g) slivered almonds
¼ cup (25g) cocoa powder

PREPARATION TIME 35 minutes
COOKING TIME 50 minutes (plus cooling time)
MAKES 60

Method

1. Preheat oven to moderate (180°C).
2. Whisk sugar and eggs in medium bowl. Stir in sifted flour, baking powder and nuts; mix to a sticky dough.
3. Knead dough on lightly floured surface until smooth. Divide dough into two portions. Using floured hands, knead one portion on lightly floured surface until smooth, but still slightly sticky. Divide this portion into four pieces.
4. Roll each piece into 25cm log shape. Knead remaining portion with cocoa until smooth, divide into two pieces. Roll each piece of chocolate mixture into a 25cm log shape.
5. Place one chocolate log on lightly greased oven tray. Place a plain log on each side, press gently together to form a slightly flattened shape. Repeat with remaining logs.
6. Bake in moderate oven (180°C) about 30 minutes or until browned lightly. Cool on tray 10 minutes.
7. Reduce oven to slow (150°C).
8. Using a serrated knife, cut logs diagonally into 5mm slices. Place slices in a single layer on ungreased oven trays.
9. Bake in slow oven (150°C) about 20 minutes or until dry and crisp, turning over halfway through cooking; cool on wire racks.

TIP Store biscotti in an airtight container for up to four weeks. Not suitable to freeze.

mini florentines

These rich little morsels are quick to mix, look very pretty, and will always be appreciated at an indulgent afternoon tea.

Ingredients

¾ cup (120g) sultanas
2 cups (80g) corn flakes
¾ cup (60g) flaked almonds, roasted
½ cup (110g) red glacé cherries
⅔ cup (160ml) sweetened condensed milk
60g white eating chocolate, melted
60g dark eating chocolate, melted

PREPARATION TIME 10 minutes
COOKING TIME 6 minutes per tray (plus cooling time)
MAKES 45

Method

1. Preheat oven to moderate (180°C).
2. Combine sultanas, corn flakes, nuts, cherries and condensed milk in medium bowl.
3. Drop heaped teaspoons of mixture onto baking-paper-lined oven trays, allowing 5cm between each florentine.
4. Bake in moderate oven (180°C) about 6 minutes or until browned lightly. Cool on trays.
5. Spread half of the bases with white chocolate and remaining half with dark chocolate; run fork through chocolate to make waves. Allow chocolate to set at room temperature.

Corn flakes are an essential ingredient in these little gourmet biscuits, so make sure they are fresh.

TIP Florentines can be stored in an airtight container for up to two weeks. Not suitable to freeze.

gourmet rocky road

This version of the well-known sweet is a shimmer of white chocolate and marshmallow, with an exotic twist of turkish delight and pistachios.

Ingredients

300g toasted marshmallow with coconut, chopped coarsely

400g turkish delight, chopped coarsely

¼ cup (40g) roasted blanched almonds, chopped coarsely

½ cup (75g) shelled pistachios, roasted

450g white eating chocolate, melted

PREPARATION TIME 25 minutes (plus refrigeration time)
MAKES 30 (more if the pieces are cut smaller)

Method

1. Grease two 8cm x 26cm bar cake pans; line base and sides with baking paper, extending paper 5cm above long sides.

2. Combine marshmallow, turkish delight and nuts in large bowl. Working quickly, stir in chocolate; spread mixture into prepared pans, push mixture down firmly to flatten the top. Refrigerate until set then cut as desired.

The marshmallow does not need to be cut up into exactly the same size. In fact, a little variety in the size of the pieces adds to the finish.

TIP

To get a nice clean edge when you cut the rocky road, run the knife under hot water, wipe it dry, then use it to make one or two cuts. Repeat the process to do more cutting. The idea is to always cut with a warm, dry knife.

almond nougat

A gift of homemade nougat is something very special.
This recipe is flavoured with honey and almonds, in the
classic European style.

Ingredients

2 sheets rice paper (confectionery rice
    paper)
½ cup (175g) honey
1⅓ cups (300g) caster sugar
2 tablespoons water
1 egg white
2 cups (320g) blanched almonds, roasted

PREPARATION TIME 10 minutes (plus standing time)
COOKING TIME 30 minutes
MAKES 49

Method

1. Lightly grease a deep 15cm-square cake pan. Trim one sheet of rice paper into a 15cm square; line base of pan.
2. Combine honey, sugar and water in small saucepan; stir over heat, without boiling, until sugar dissolves. Using a pastry brush dipped in hot water, brush down the side of the pan to dissolve any sugar crystals; bring to a boil. Boil, uncovered, without stirring, about 10 minutes or until syrup reaches 164°C on the candy thermometer; remove pan immediately from heat. Place thermometer in pan of boiling water; remove from heat to allow thermometer to gradually decrease in temperature.
3. Beat egg white in small heatproof bowl with electric mixer until soft peaks form. With motor operating, add hot syrup to egg white in a thin, steady stream.
4. Stir almonds into egg white mixture; spoon into prepared pan. Press mixture firmly into pan. Cut remaining sheet of rice paper large enough to cover top of nougat; press lightly onto nougat. Stand about 2 hours or until cool; cut into 2cm squares.

TIPS

• It is important to use a candy thermometer in this recipe in order to get the correct consistency when making the nougat.
• The nougat must be left to cool at room temperature, as refrigeration makes it soften. It's best to store the nougat in an airtight container at room temperature.
• Rice paper is a fine, edible paper made in Holland. It is sold in specialist food stores and some delicatessens. It is not the same as the Asian rice papers used in Vietnamese dishes.

gift baskets

equipment

A NEW HOME, A NEW BABY, A BIRTHDAY… there are so many reasons to give presents, and a gift becomes wonderfully personal when the items gathered are put together with thought and purpose. This requires a little planning, so your first tool in the exercise will actually be pencil and paper. Jot down details of your friend – what they do and what they like. DECIDE ON A THEME FOR THE GIFT BASKET, AND MAKE A LIST OF EVERYTHING YOU THINK IS NEEDED. The next step is to buy your pieces. Allow yourself a little time to do this, so you can find that perfect item. You should also work out how you will assemble the gifts into a beautiful package. You could FIND INSPIRATION FLICKING THROUGH THE PAGES OF A GLOSSY MAGAZINE, where professional stylists have created beautiful arrangements of objects. You could also borrow ideas from displays in shop windows. Finally, compose a message to accompany your gift. IT REALLY IS THE THOUGHT THAT COUNTS.

CONTAINERS

Rather than put the items in a cheap cane basket, which someone then has to stow or throw away, make the container as important a part of the gift as everything else. A large mixing bowl may hold gear for the kitchen; a small toy box could be filled with gifts for a child, or a plant pot with the makings of a herb garden. The container itself should be able to be used again, so find the most beautiful example you can. Your friend will appreciate your gift even more if you make it practical as well as pretty.

SOFT PACKAGING

Good packing means keeping items snugly in place and to do this you need something soft to stuff the gaps. Instead of going down the route of wads of tissue paper, use some fabric items to do the same job. Tea-towels or hand towels may be rolled into cylinders and tied with ribbon, or be piled in a stack to fill up a larger space. For smaller gaps, use the towels individually. As before, the emphasis is on including things that may be reused, rather than having a lot of excess packaging that will only be thrown away.

CARDS & TAGS

The message on a card can be as enjoyable as the gift, so put a little time into its presentation. There are many lovely cards and envelopes available, or you could make your own (see page 66) in colours that match the other items in the gift. Remember, making a card can be as simple as sticking a square of pretty paper on a tag. Work out the exact wording of your message before transcribing it on the card; you don't want any crossing out. And make sure you use a pen that writes well.

TRIM & RIBBON

To pretty up your parcel, use some of the many ribbons and braid trims that are now available. Tying a present with a big luscious bow may seem a little corny, but it's one of the fastest ways to announce the arrival of a gift. There are many internet sites with instructions on making bows – simply type "how to tie a bow" in your preferred search engine. For a feature bow, you could use wired ribbon, which has a tiny wire along each edge that gives a bow more body. Use unwired ribbon to tie together towels and other objects in your gift arrangement.

new home

It's the small things that help transform a new house into a home. Focusing on items for just one room makes assembling the gift hamper more manageable.

Items

colander

kitchen apron

flour-sack tea-towels (these durable yet soft tea-towels have a fine even weave similar to the feed-sack towels of the 1930s)

selection of wooden utensils

wooden pepper grinder

glass bottles filled with oil and vinegar

fresh rosemary, picked from the garden and tied with string (this flavoursome herb also signifies remembrance)

Method

Moving house is a major event, and as the kitchen is the heart of the home, putting together a gift pack especially for that room will mean a lot for its recipient. Assemble items that are both practical and beautiful. They will be used every day, so quality is important. Look in specialist kitchenware outlets or at chefs' suppliers for sturdy utensils: wooden spoons with good thick handles, a solid cook's knife, cake tins and cookie cutters in a range of shapes and sizes. Source thick linen or cotton tea-towels in a classic design; they will last for years.

You could add some condiments to make those first few meals at the new home more of a gourmet event. Include in your gift pack grinders filled with peppercorns and rock salt, or a mortar and pestle and a selection of spices packed in small matching jars. Top-quality extra-virgin olive oil and an aged vinegar will be welcome, too. Package your items in a practical container: a colander (as used here), a large pan, a wok or a big mixing bowl would all be suitable. And every time your friends use your gifts, they will remember they came from you.

craft starter box

A colourful collection of fabric pieces, threads, yarn and buttons will be happily received by someone keen on craft, whether they're a novice or an experienced hand.

Items

gift box, available from newsagencies
    and specialist card or paper shops
glass jars
buttons and ribbons
selection of fabric pieces
thread, pins, needles
tape measure
scissors
woollen yarn
pair of knitting needles

Method

This box is packed with a gorgeous array of sewing and craft materials to gladden the heart of a craft fan. There is a selection of fabric lengths that are suitable for small projects or for being made into patchwork squares. Quilters will appreciate a selection of fat quarters, which are sold pre-cut at larger fabric outlets and specialist quilting suppliers.

The buttons and ribbons could be used to brighten cushions or be incorporated into a scrapbooking project. The pretty selection of woollen yarns could be knitted up into a scarf or a hat.

This is a particularly good idea for a young craft enthusiast, who will love the assortment of patterns and colours. And it comes already organised in its own storage container.

TIP

If you know someone is especially keen on a craft such as cross stitch or knitting, you could make up a package with everything in it to complete a particular project. Youngsters and novices will appreciate receiving a basic guide to crafts or a list of good craft websites. Very useful for basics is www.craftown.com.

new baby hamper

The arrival of a little person after so many months is reason to celebrate. Wrap a combination of practical and indulgent items to help out the busy new parents.

Items

wooden toy-box
teddy bears
baby instruction manual
face washers
muslin wraps
nappies, both cloth and disposable, wrapped in a ribbon
baby singlets
organic skincare lotions for baby
soothing lotion for the skin
handmade "Babysitting" voucher
celebratory champagne

Method

There are so many products for new babies it can seem overwhelming. But a parcel of basic baby equipment, all suitable to be thrown in the wash and tumble-dried, is a thoughtful gift. You can be sure that baby singlets, nappies (both cloth and disposable), and muslin wraps will all be used.

Be luxurious in your choice of skincare lotions. There are some wonderful products based on pure, organic ingredients that also incorporate aromatherapy oils to soothe both babies and their sleep-deprived parents. Look for ones specially formulated for newborns. Splash out on some celebratory champagne for your friends – even a breastfeeding mum can have a little after three months. Write up a voucher with an offer to babysit, too, or to make the parents a gourmet dinner. Allowing your friends to take a break may be the present they appreciate most of all.

TIP

With so many beautiful things around for babies, it's tempting to splash out on a bundle of cute outfits. If you do buy clothes, make sure they can be machine washed in warm water and tumble dried. Also, buy a size or two larger than what baby is wearing now. It's a relief for parents to have something on hand for their little one to grow into.

garden pack

Giving a gift that grows is a lovely thought. Assemble everything needed for a friend to nurture a patch of green in their home.

Items

glazed terracotta pot
a beautiful book on gardening
watering can
selection of seeds and bulbs packed in
   glass jars
gardening gloves
garden fork and hand trowel
a gardener's hand cream

Method

Gathered here are good-quality tools, a terracotta pot, seeds and a beautiful book of gardens so your friend can dream of what might be achieved. There is also a pack of gardener's hand cream; digging in the soil is drying on hands.

Tailor your choices to what your friend likes and where they live. If they are very busy, provide a selection of succulents that need only a little care. For a keen cook, present the beginnings of a herb garden. For someone who lives in an apartment, choose seeds for colourful balcony plants.

Present this gift with a bag of potting mix and a promise to visit to see the results.

TIP
Write down for your friend any special tips for growing the seeds you have given them. For example, the tulip bulbs included here should be stored in a brown paper bag in the crisper drawer of the fridge for six to seven weeks before they are planted out. This reproduces the frigid conditions of a northern hemisphere winter, and enables the bulbs to produce a very strong flowering shoot.

destress & relax

Anyone would love to receive this package. It gives them permission to relax, to spoil themselves, to take some time that's just for them.

Items

galvanised tub

a beautiful book to flick through (shown is *Australian House & Garden Sanctuary*, from ACP Books)

oil burner and essential oil

organic tea

bath towels

bubble bath

hydrating face spray

CD of relaxing music

loofah and shower mitt

handmade "Massage" voucher

Method

This lovely gift includes everything needed for a relaxing foot bath – even the basin for your friend to soak their feet in. There is something to soothe every one of the five senses: calming music, a soothing blend of essential oils for aromatherapy, lemongrass tea to cleanse the palate, bubble bath and a written promise for a massage, and a book that is beautiful to look at.

Scent has a powerful effect on your mood, because the part of your brain that processes smell is close to the limbic system, which controls your emotions. Fragrances such as lavender, rose and vanilla have long been celebrated for their relaxing properties, so include products with these scents in your package.

You could even make up your own relaxing blend of essential oils to use in an oil burner (four drops patchouli, two drops orange, two drops sandalwood); alternatively, buy a bottle of pre-blended oils to give to your friend.

But perhaps the best thing about this package is the idea behind it – that you are giving someone the excuse to sit and simply relax and enjoy themselves for a precious hour.

TIP

A handful of marbles added to a footbath is a clever idea for a DIY foot massage. Just rub your feet over the marbles for a wonderfully soothing sensation.

garden

equipment

Borrowing beauty from nature makes a home sing. Flowers and fragrances have a way of reaching to the soul and there are few people who remain untouched by THE LOVELINESS OF A CARED-FOR GARDEN. A green thumb is certainly something to be admired, and for keen gardeners we have projects that add to the appeal of an outdoor space. But if you are less of a gardener, there are other ways to BRING FLOWERS INTO YOUR LIFE. A selection of flowers from a shop may be arranged into bunches. A bloom from a bouquet may be pressed, and store-bought herbs may be made into sachets. IT'S WONDERFUL TO NURTURE FLOWERS AND HERBS YOURSELF, but there is also nothing wrong with buying them – the pleasure you gain is just as genuine.

FLORIST'S WIRE

This wire is available in several gauges and may be fabric-covered or not. It's often sold on spools at craft stores, though the heavier wire may come in cut lengths. It's relatively easy to twist, but you will need wire cutters to snip it; scissors are not recommended. Its advantage is that it doesn't cut into plants in the same way as other wire. It is used by florists to wire stems upright in arrangements.

FLOWER PRESS

A traditional flower press has layers of blotting paper and cardboard, with wooden covers at the top and bottom. Flowers are placed on the blotting paper and screws or straps are used to tighten the press, drawing more moisture from the flowers. The plant material may be left to dry from 10 days to three weeks. There is also a Microfleur microwave flower press, which allows you to dry flowers in minutes in a microwave oven. The flowers are placed between fabric-lined felt pads inside the press's plastic covers. Drying is done in short bursts in the microwave oven.

SECATEURS

These are designed for small cutting jobs in the garden, but the blade must be sharp or the secateurs will tear a branch rather than cut it. Once a month, rub the blade over a sharpening stone (these are available from good hardware stores) to keep the cutting edge keen. Make sure the secateurs are the right size; you must be able to open and close them easily with one hand. To avoid spreading a disease from one plant to another, wipe the secateurs with a little methylated spirits between plants. For a more thorough clean, scrub the tool with warm, soapy water, dry thoroughly with a cloth and spray any metal parts with lubricating oil to prevent rust.

OASIS FOAM

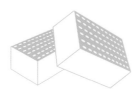

Oasis is the proprietary name for a green floral foam that holds 40 times its weight in water. The phenolic foam has an open cell structure which resembles that of cells in a plant stem; capillary action draws water through the foam. Available from craft stores, it's a great help in flower arrangements as it holds flowers in place securely. The Oasis may be contained in a rigid plastic base or have a backing material. Just remember that the floral foam is not a substitute for water; you will still need to replace the liquid drunk by the plants. Top up the water in the display container every day.

GARDEN TROWEL

This little hand tool is not at all glamorous, but it is indispensable for digging smaller holes and potting plants. The spade section is traditionally made of metal, but there are also garden trowels made of polypropylene. It's essential that the spade section is strong so it's not bent out of shape by the pressure of the dirt. Make sure the trowel is clean before you put it away; soapy water will remove mud and any sap. And pay some attention to the wooden handle; rub it with linseed oil to keep it smooth and prevent cracking.

OPAQUE CONTAINERS

Sunlight and air may be essential for growing plants, but they also hasten the breaking down of plant material. Dried herbs should be kept in opaque containers to preserve their essential oils and colour. In a similar way, pressed flowers should be stored away from the light to preserve their colours.

LAVENDER IN A TEA-LIGHT HOLDER
Choose a tea-light holder with a handle. Place over a door handle,
then half-fill with water – take a bottle of water with you to do this.
Arrange a freshly picked bunch of lavender in the container.

doorstep bouquets

Leaving a posy of flowers at someone's door is a charming way to say welcome home. They are a universal token of love and a gift filled with affection.

Materials

clean, sharp secateurs
plastic bucket
display container
bleach
bottled or filtered water
sachets of flower food (preservative available from florists and some craft suppliers)

Method

1. Select flowers that are firm and plump on clean, unbroken stems. Any discoloured leaves show that the plant, and therefore the flower, is unhealthy. Any buds you pick should be showing colour. If you're selecting flowers from your garden, cut with clean secateurs in the morning, before the heat of the day.

2. Storage containers must be clean, as bacteria can clog the stem of a plant, stopping water getting to the flower head and shortening the life of your arrangement. Scrub a plastic bucket and your preferred flower container with detergent and rinse thoroughly. Rinse again with a mild bleach solution (one cap per 3.5 litres of water).

3. Fill the clean plastic bucket half-full with bottled or filtered water; the chemicals and minerals in some tap water can also clog the stem. Add the exact amount of flower food (available from florists and some craft stores) required for the liquid; follow the instructions on the pack.

4. Trim any damaged flowers or leaves, and remove lower leaves from the stems. Half-fill a clean sink with water. Making the stem ends even, hold them under the water and cut 2.5cm from the end with sharp secateurs. Cutting them under water stops air entering the stem and blocking the water flow.

5. Transfer flowers to the storage bucket and store out of the sun in a ventilated space for six hours or overnight. This will give the blooms a good drink and infuse them with the flower food.

6. To make your posy, hold the flowers in one hand and arrange them so they look good from all angles. Trim ends under water, as before, so they are the right length for the display container (if you're using one). Mix a solution of flower food and bottled or distilled water, and add to the clean display container along with the flowers.

TIP Some of these hanging bouquets are in containers that hold water, others are not. Either way, flowers that are well hydrated before they are made into a posy will last longer.

POSY IN PAPER

Arrange flowers in a posy – we used dahlias and lisianthus. Wrap water-soaked paper towel around the end of the stems, and secure with an elastic band or florist's wire. Wrap clear cellophane around the posy's base, then wrap the posy in crisp brown paper, securing the paper in place with pearl-headed pins. Carefully thread a long piece of florist's wire around the back of the flowers to use as a hanging loop.

FLOWERS IN FRENCH MARKET BAG

Choose a suitable large bag. Cut off the top of a large plastic drink bottle, then half-fill the bottle with water. Make your posy – we used fragrant stocks and roses – and place in the water container, then put into the basket. If you are worried about spillages, place a plastic bag over the bottle base, and tape the top of the bag around the flower stems.

BOUQUET WITH TWINE

Arrange the flowers and secure in place with an elastic band. Wind garden twine around the bouquet in neat rows to cover the elastic band, then tie in a knot or bow. Use hardy flowers as they will not be in water until your friend arrives home. We chose drought-resistant proteas and included gum leaves for a beautiful scent.

FLOWERS IN LACY JARS

Cut a length of lace curtaining to fit a clean jar. Spray lace with repositionable spray adhesive and wrap around the jar. Spray-paint white gloss over the lace and, when the paint's dry, remove the lace. Cut a length of wire and use pliers to tie it around the jar's mouth. Cut another wire length to make a hanging loop and twist it onto the wire on the jar. We hung three jars at different lengths. Fill with water and add hyacinths, bud roses, geraniums and freesias.

HYDRANGEAS IN A HEART

Gather some lichen-covered twigs, and include some longer lengths. Gather in a bunch and tie at the base with florist's wire. Bend over the longer twigs into a heart shape, and secure the thin ends at the bottom. Weave the stems of a few heads of hydrangeas into the twigs. Place florist's water vials on the ends of the hydrangea stems to keep them fresh. Tie a ribbon in a bow at the base of the arrangement. Use fishing line to hang the wreath from the door.

FRANGIPANI IN A WATERING CAN

This is a very simple idea. Fill a galvanised watering can with water, arrange flowers and leave on the doorstep. We used frangipani branch cuttings, which make a great gift as your friend can plant them in their own garden or pot. Frangipani doesn't need water if you are going to strike it, as it likes to dry out a little before being put in the soil. Wrap the end of the frangipani stem in a plastic bag as the sap can be sticky and messy.

drying garden herbs

Garden herbs may be used fresh, but if you dry the leaves they can be stored all year in the kitchen cupboard and also used for projects other than cooking.

Materials

Except for lavender, you should harvest herbs for drying just before they flower. This is when they have the most oil, the most flavour and the most fragrance. If you're not sure of the flowering season, look for buds as a guide. (Herbs that have flowered may still be dried.)

LAVENDER HERB PILLOWS, SEE 143 FOR INSTRUCTIONS

TIP

The best herbs for air-drying are the "sturdy", low-moisture herbs such as sage, thyme, oregano, parsley and lavender. "Tender-leaf" herbs with a higher moisture content, such as basil, tarragon, mint or lemon balm, should be hung in smaller bunches so they dry quickly and don't become mouldy, or be oven-dried. Do not use pesticides on herbs.

Method

1. Cut the herbs in the mid morning, when the dew has dried on the leaves, but before the afternoon heat. Use secateurs or sharp scissors to snip off branches. Discard damaged or old leaves.

2. Rinse each branch with cold water, then dry with paper towel. The herbs must be totally dry. Any moisture will encourage mould, which can destroy an entire bunch of herbs.

3. To air-dry herbs: remove leaves along the lower stems; they are not as potent as leaves near the buds. Gather five or six stems in a small bunch and tie stems together. Place upside-down in a large paper bag with several holes punched or cut in it for ventilation. The herb leaves should not touch the side of the bag. Gather the paper bag around the stems and secure with a rubber band. Leave in a warm, dry spot for two weeks or longer.

4. When leaves are dry and crumble easily, they are ready to store. If there are any signs of mould, throw away the entire bunch. Coarsely crumble off the herbs into a container.

5. To oven-dry herbs: remove the best leaves from the stems. Lay leaves on a paper towel on an oven tray; their edges should not touch. Lay another piece of paper towel on top, then more leaves. Up to five layers may be dried at once. Place in an electric stove with the oven light on, or in a gas stove with the pilot light on, and leave to dry overnight. This is the best method for drying leaves separately and works very well for mint, sage and bay leaf.

6. Place dried herbs in opaque, airtight containers and store in a cool, dry place. It is best to finely crumble them just before using.

SMALL BUNCHES
Gather only five or six stems in each bunch. The paper bag must be large enough for the herbs not to touch its sides.

VENTILATION
Put holes in the paper bag for ventilation. Drying herbs in a bag protects them from dust.

OVEN DRYING HERBS
Oven drying is particularly good for mint, sage and bay leaves. Ensure that the edges of the leaves do not touch.

STORAGE
Dried herbs should be stored in opaque containers in a cool place, as heat and light break down the oils.

herb sachets

Herb sachets popped in the drawer or hung in a wardrobe are a gentle way to repel insects or give your clothing a pleasant scent.

Materials

Moth-repellent mix
(enough for two sachets)
¼ cup (10g) dried tansy
¼ cup (15g) dried thyme
¼ cup (10g) dried mint
¼ cup (20g) dried wormwood
2 cinnamon sticks, crumbled

Scented sachet mix
1 tablespoon (about 5g) dried lemon balm
2 tablespoons (about 10g) dried lavender
2 tablespoons (about 10g) dried thyme

For the sachet
herb filling of your choice
2 x 12cm squares cotton organdie
13cm x 30cm piece of fabric, for the cover
35cm ribbon, 5mm wide
butterfly motifs (three 2.5cm appliqué
 butterflies, and 1 guipure lace butterfly,
 5.5cm x 4.5cm), optional
stranded embroidery thread, optional
pinking shears

Method

1. Mix all the herb ingredients in a large bowl.
2. Using a 1cm seam, stitch organdie squares together, leaving a 3cm opening. Trim across corners diagonally, then turn right-way out.
3. Fill with your desired herbal mix. An easy way to do this is to form a piece of paper into a cone, put its end in the bag's opening, and spoon in the herbs. Stitch closed.
4. Hem the 13cm ends of the cover fabric. Turn them over twice, then pin and stitch in place.
5. Fold fabric into thirds so the middle section is 10cm across. Mark the edges of the front with pins. If you are adding butterfly motifs and stitching (see template on page 177), lightly mark their positions with a pencil. Sew motifs in place, then with three strands of embroidery cotton work small running stitches over the pattern.
6. Refold fabric into thirds, with wrong sides facing. On the back, fold the top section under by 4cm or so. Press, then allowing 1.5cm at the top and bottom, pin and baste together, then stitch. Remove basting.
7. Using pinking shears, trim top and bottom edges to 1cm. If you are adding ribbon, fold length in half and stitch in place. Trim ribbon ends with a diagonal cut. Slide herb sachet into the cover.

TIP
These herbs are noted for their insect-repelling properties: lavender, wormwood, pennyroyal, rue, mint, tansy and rosemary. Cinnamon or cloves add a pleasant scent to the mix.

IN THE MIX
Wormwood and tansy are quite pungent herbs, so sweeten the mix by adding cinnamon or cloves.

SACHET COVER
Fold over the top section of the cover's back by 4cm or so to give yourself room to slide in the herb sachet. When those herbs lose their potency, pop in a sachet of new herbs.

GIVE A SELECTION
Make up different selections of herbs to fill the sachets. A mix of lemon balm and lavender gives a scent that is very appealing.

scented pillows

Lavender pillows are a traditional way to promote rest, and a little lavender bear may help soothe a child to sleep.

Lavender herb pillow

Materials

Lavender mix
½ cup (30g) dried lavender buds
¾ cup linseeds (flax seeds)

For the pillow
2 pieces 15cm x 17cm cotton organdie (or similar fine cotton fabric)
15cm x 39cm piece of fabric, for the cover
soft pencil
DMC stranded embroidery cotton in Ecru, Very Dark Cranberry (600) and Cranberry (603) (optional)
embroidery needle
trim for flap (optional)
press stud

Method

1. Mix lavender and linseeds in a bowl.
2. Using 1.5cm seams stitch together organdie pieces, leaving a 5cm opening. Trim corners. Turn right-way out. Fill with mix; stitch closed.
3. Machine stitch a 5mm hem on one short end of cover fabric.
4. Lay out cover fabric. Mark a vertical line 8cm from the unhemmed short edge; mark the centre of the edge. Draw from this point to the top and bottom of the line, marking out the flap. Trim fabric to flap lines.
5. Turn under a flap edge by 1cm, press and stitch. Repeat on other edge.
6. Add trim to flap (if using). Mark any embroidery and work stitches. We did rows of chain and running stitch, using three strands of thread.
7. Using 1.5cm seams and with wrong sides facing, sew a bag 15cm long to the bottom edge of the flap. Neaten side seams.
8. Sew press stud under flap. Place sachet in cover. See photo, page 138.

Lavender bear

Materials

1 piece white felt (approximately 31cm x 23cm, available at craft stores)
stranded embroidery cotton in pale yellow, dark brown and light brown
embroidery needle
a little over ½ cup (about 30g) dried lavender buds

FILLING WITH HERBS
The easiest way to add herbs to your projects is to spoon them into a paper funnel and tap them down.

Method

1. Trace or photocopy the bear template on page 177. Cut out two bear shapes from the felt.
2. Using a soft pencil or dressmaker's carbon, mark the face and stitch outline on one of the bear shapes.
3. Using straight stitches, work the pattern for the bear's face. We used four strands of light brown cotton for the bear's eyes and mouth, and both light and dark brown cotton on the nose. Complete the bear's mouth by working one lot of running stitch, then working another lot to fill in the gaps and make a continuous line of stitching.
4. Join the bear shapes. Using six strands of yellow embroidery thread, work the stitch outline on the bear's body with two lots of running stitch, as you did for the mouth. Sew until there is a 6cm opening left.
5. Fill the bear with lavender. Form a piece of paper into a cone, put its end in the opening, and shake in the lavender. Use the end of a teaspoon to push the lavender into the arms and legs. Finish the stitching and secure the thread with two or three backstitches.

bamboo edging

Give hedges or garden beds a geometric finish with this decorative edging of bamboo. It also looks cute lining the edge of a path.

Materials

lengths of bamboo slats, 50–60mm wide (look for them at nurseries, craft stores or bamboo suppliers)
twine for tying
hacksaw or sharp secateurs to cut bamboo
bird decoration (optional)

Method

1. Measure the length and height of the hedge or garden bed to be edged, to determine how much bamboo you will need. For this 30cm high hedge, we formed 60cm long bamboo pieces into arches about 20cm high and 30cm wide. Bamboo is often sold in quite long lengths, about 2.7 metres, so cut these in half.

2. Soak the bamboo lengths in water overnight to make them easier to bend. We tied ours in a bundle and dropped them into a swimming pool overnight.

3. Cut the desired length (we cut ours into 60cm sections) with a small hacksaw or sharp garden secateurs.

4. Gently pre-bend the bamboo into an arch. It's easiest to work gently from one end, rather than holding both ends of the bamboo and trying to bend it in one action.

5. Poke each end of the arch about 5cm into the ground. Complete the first row of arches.

6. Add another row of bamboo arches, starting halfway across the first arch you made.

7. Use good-quality twine to tie the first and second rows together where the arches meet. This is for decoration only. We added a little blue bird just for fun.

A small hacksaw blade is good for cutting the bamboo into the desired lengths. Along with the bamboo and twine, it's all you need for this project.

ALTERNATIVE

You can also use lengths of cane, available from craft stores, to make a garden edging. Having three rows of cane arches, in three heights, looks very effective.

pressing flowers

It's been a tradition since Victorian times to catch the colours of spring by pressing flowers. You could even preserve a flower taken from a wedding bouquet or a Valentine's gift as a romantic keepsake.

Items

flowers
flower press (either traditional or
    microwave) or a heavy book
    with tissue paper
magnetic Perspex frames, to display
    the flowers (optional)

Method

1. A simple way to press flowers is by putting them between the pages of a heavy book. Place the flowers in a single layer between tissue paper; they must not overlap. Close the book, place some more on top for added weight, and leave for at least a week.

2. A traditional flower press has layers of blotting paper and cardboard to draw moisture from plant material. Straps or screws are used to tighten the press and extract more moisture. Several layers of flowers, on separate pieces of blotting paper, may be pressed at the one time. Follow the instructions on your flower press, and leave the flowers for 10 days to three weeks.

3. A fast method of pressing flowers is in a microwave flower press. This is also a good way to preserve a flower's colour. There is a danger you may scorch the flower, so do a few practise runs first.

Place the flowers between the pads on the microwave press (shown is a Microfleur press) and clip the covers in place. Dry the flowers using short bursts on High. Use an initial burst of about 45 seconds for 600W ovens, 30 seconds for 750W and 20 seconds for 900W ovens. Follow with shorter bursts, half to one-third as long as the initial one. Refer to the press's instructions for detailed information.

4. Display the flowers in a Perspex frame, as shown here, or use them in another project.

PRESSING IN A BOOK
This is an easy and popular way to press flowers. Simply place between tissue paper in a heavy book and leave. The flowers should not overlap.

TRADITIONAL PRESS
Sheets of blotting paper and cardboard are used in a traditional flower press. Several lots of flowers may be pressed between the different layers at the one time.

MICROWAVE PRESS
Using a microwave flower press is fast; it's also good for preserving the colours of the flowers.

  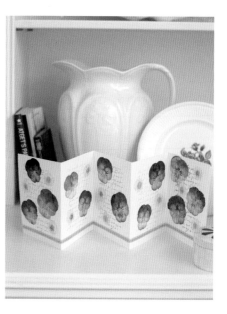

To make the pansy card, glue together two three-fold cards with acid-free adhesive to make a five-panel concertina card. Press under books until adhesive dries. Ink the script stamp with either navy blue or sepia acid-free ink. Stamp it twice on scrap card before applying to the concertina card. Use the navy blue and sepia on alternate sections. Clean and dry the stamp between colours.

Place pansies and yellow Marguerite daisies on card to get an idea of their final position. Apply adhesive to decorative ribbon (buy 1 metre) and glue along the bottom of the card. Refold card and press under books until the adhesive dries.

Lay pansies face down on newspaper. Using an acid-free spray adhesive, spray lightly over the flowers. Hold the can at least 20cm above the flowers so the spray doesn't flip them over. Use tweezers to gently lift and place flowers on card.

Repeat the gluing process with the yellow Marguerite daisies and leave until the adhesive is dry. Carefully refold card. Alternatively, instead of spray adhesive, you could use PVA, watered down and applied lightly with a brush to each flower. It's important the adhesive is all over the flowers as the petals have a tendency to curl.

NOTE Pressed flowers lose their colour over time, especially if exposed to strong sunlight. Beginners will have most success pressing flowers with a single layer of petals. As you become more experienced, you may dismantle a flower so it lies flat for drying, then reassemble it on a picture. Use a clear-drying, acid-free adhesive to glue flowers. Most PVA craft glues are suitable. Apply the glue with a fine brush or toothpick to the backs of petals.

Opposite: Pressed flowers may be incorporated into cards, but they must be handled gently. Choose a cardstock that complements the flower's colour. You can add depth to your design by stamping on a background pattern, gluing on ribbon or colouring the edges of the card with acid-free chalk.

teepee planter

Even a novice could attempt this gorgeous teepee planter. There is nothing tricky, just pruned twigs made into a teepee, and a beautiful climbing plant.

Materials

seven 1.8-metre lengths of tree prunings (we used peach blossom)
secateurs
florist's wire

Method

1. Prepare seven 1.8 metre lengths of tree prunings by clipping off the side branches with secateurs. Save the longer clippings (those longer than 30cm) to create the spiral.
2. Place the thick ends of the 1.8-metre lengths in the ground in a circle, evenly spaced, and using florist's wire, tie the top together like a teepee.
3. Working from the base, wind the 30cm lengths in and out of the tepee supports until you have made a complete circle. Use florist's wire to secure the lengths as you go.
4. Start the upward spiral by adding more branches of uneven lengths and wiring into place. Stagger the ends so that each twig stops and starts at random intervals.
5. Bind the bundle together regularly with florist's wire to ensure strength and stability.
6. Keep spiralling upwards, adding more twigs until you reach the top, then bind the lot together to the original tie in Step 2.
7. Plant with climbing plants such as sweetpeas, peas or beans.

EASY ALTERNATIVE

If there are no prunings available, you may construct this planter using bamboo garden stakes for the vertical supports, and cane from a craft store for the spiral.

Use secateurs to neatly clip off side branches from the tree pruning. Save those that are 30cm or longer.

Set up your teepee shape, evenly spacing the thicker ends of the branches in the ground. Use a small garden trowel to help dig the holes.

Wind the 30cm lengths in and out until you have made a complete circle, then tie with the florist's wire. The circle should have about seven strands.

Start winding the thinner branches up into a spiral. Add in another branch at random intervals, binding it into the bundle with the wire.

You need to bind the bundle of branches regularly with the wire to make the planter strong.

When the spiral reaches the top, bind it to the teepee supports with the florist's wire.

flower chandelier

A hanging globe of blooms is a delightful idea for a party or even a wedding at home. It takes a little patience, but the effect is spectacular.

Materials

12cm diameter Oasis ball (floral foam ball), available from florist or craft suppliers

45cm length florist's wire (or 22 gauge wire)

60cm double-sided satin ribbon, 24mm wide (the length will vary, depending on where you want to hang the ball)

Sim carnations, 30 stems

baby's breath (perennial gypsophila), 1 bunch

secateurs

Method

1. Float the Oasis ball on a bucket of water and leave it to sink. This will take a couple of minutes. Do not push it down as this traps air, rather than water, inside.

2. Bend the florist's wire in half and push the sharp ends right through the Oasis, leaving the loop poking out at the top. Bend the ends back and push into the Oasis.

3. Cut carnations and baby's breath so at least 1cm of stem remains. Work out where the centre of the ball is and push in a large flower to mark the spot. Then, moving vertically, push in a line of carnations right around the Oasis ball. Your aim is to mark the ball in half vertically. Push in the flowers as far as they will go.

4. Push in a line of baby's breath next to the carnations, then a line of carnations. Continue in this way until one half of the ball is covered.

5. Thread ribbon through the wire and knot it in place. Hang the ball, then pull around the ribbon so its knot is near the wire loop, hidden by the flowers. Finish pushing in the flowers on the other side.

MAKE THE WIRE LOOP
Bend the florist's wire into a hairpin shape and push its straight ends right through the oasis ball. The loop will poke out the top. Bend the straight ends back against the ball.

INSERTING FLOWERS
Push in the flowers as far as they will go. If they are at all loose, they may fall out.

ALTERNATIVES
Any flower with a firm stem may be used in a hanging arrangement. Roses, hydrangeas, lisianthus and even lavender look wonderful displayed in this way.

home

equipment

Thinking of DIY may conjure images of people wearing overalls and carrying an electric drill, but you don't need to have a home workshop to complete these projects. All you need is a place where they can be left undisturbed to dry. ALL THE PROJECTS IN THIS CHAPTER CAN BE FINISHED IN A DAY OR A WEEKEND, and they turn basic items into something far more beautiful. Frames and noticeboards are made glamorous, and a table is transformed from purely practical to appealing. And what's needed for this to happen? LITTLE MORE THAN PATIENCE, a hammer and a paintbrush. Take a look and be inspired.

HAMMER

The claw hammer is familiar to most people. It has a slightly rounded, hardened face and a claw at its back for levering out nails. Hammers are sized by the weight of the head, and claw hammers tend to be sized from 450-570g for bench work, and from 620-680g for building work. A smaller tack hammer or cross-pein (Warrington) hammer is useful for lighter jobs like driving in tacks. The hammer's rounded face prevents damage to the nail's head, but for more delicate operations, buffer the blows by covering the hammer with a wad of fabric, held in place with a rubber band.

SCREWDRIVERS

There are three basic types of tip on screwdrivers: slotted, which means a flat blade that fits standard screws; Phillips, a cross-shape for screws with recessed heads; and Pozi, which is angled to allow greater pressure to be applied. Screw bits fitted in an electric drill do the same job as a screwdriver. Make sure that the screwdriver blade or tip fits the screw head exactly and reaches the bottom of the slot or recess. If it's too wide it will damage the surrounding timber when you work in the screw, and if it's too narrow, it may snap or twist.

PVA GLUE

PVA (polyvinyl acetate) is the most common adhesive on the market. There are a variety of PVA formulas around, but you may find that the PVA you bought for one job is adequate for another. Have a look at the label before you decide you have to buy something else. PVA is excellent to use as a wood glue, but it will not stick non-porous materials such as plastic or glass. It needs a little pressure to stick, so glued joins should be clamped in place while it dries. It sets best at room temperature in a well-ventilated room. As PVA is water-based, you can clean brushes or wash away spills with warm soapy water.

HAND SAW

The best all-purpose saw for woodworking is the panel saw. Choose one that has a blade 550-600mm long with 10 teeth to each 25mm. After some use, the saw's teeth will need resharpening and resetting. Ask your local hardware store to recommend someone. When you have finished a job, place a protective sleeve over the saw's teeth (a piece of plastic pipe with a slit down one side is good). A hacksaw is used to cut metal and plastic pipe. Once it becomes blunt, a hacksaw's blade should be replaced as it cannot be resharpened.

PAINT & BRUSHES

Paint is either oil-based (enamel) or water-based (acrylic). Enamels are thinned with mineral turpentine, and acrylics with water. Paints with a gloss (shiny) finish are easier to clean and are good on metal. Choose a paint with a flat finish for a matt effect. Low sheen paint has a slight gloss. Using a good brush makes painting easier. Bristles must be springy, well attached and their ends finely split to carry more paint. A smaller fitch brush could be used for the projects in this book, as it allows you to paint more delicate pieces without leaving any obvious lap marks.

STAPLE GUN

A basic staple gun is adequate for the projects in this book, although there are powered models available which may be preferred by people with wrist or hand problems. A staple gun works by firing heavy metal staples into a surface, where the staples act like nails. Look for a staple gun with a rust-resistant finish and an opening so that you can see when it's low on staples. Also check if its design is meant to prevent jamming. Staple guns are most widely used by upholsterers, and you will need a heavy-duty staple gun to staple vinyl or leather.

MEASURING TAPE

A steel measuring tape has a flexible blade that retracts into a case, and most have a locking device so you can hold the tape in place if needed. A small hook riveted on the tape's end helps guide it on the object you are measuring. The tape itself is marked in millimetres, centimetres and metres, sometimes on both sides. As it's steel, the tape is easier to hold straight to get a true measure, but you must keep it dry to prevent it rusting. When working, remember the carpenter's adage: "measure twice, cut once".

joined frames

A favourite collection of photos makes a bigger impact when displayed together. Putting them in a set of joined frames ensures they will be read as a group.

Materials

4 identical purchased frames (shown are box frames by Corban and Blair)
6 mending plates with suitable screws (they're often sold in packs of 4 with screws included)
pencil
hammer and nail
screwdriver

Method

1. Line up the frames in a block, face down, with two at the top and two at the bottom.

2. Place a mending plate over where the frames join. With a pencil, mark the position of the screw holes. Use a hammer and nail to make a small starter hole, then screw the mending plate in place. Work in this order:

(a) Join the two upper frames across their base.

(b) Join the two lower frames across their top end.

(c) Join the two upper frames across their top end.

(d) Join the bases of the upper frames to the tops of the lower frames, then join the sides of the upper frames to the sides of the lower frames.

3. Place pictures in the frames and hang in place from the wires on the upper frames.

JOINING FRAMES
Do not screw in the screws too tightly, as they may pull the frames out of position.

NOTE
This is an attractive way to display any pictures with a theme. They may be photographs of your family, or a set of botanical prints, or even beautiful images cut out and kept from the pages of glossy magazines or calendars. The only thing to remember is that they all should be about the same size.

button frames

Decorating plain frames with buttons is a simple project, but the result can be quite beautiful. Use this technique on a frame for a small mirror or a family photograph.

Materials

purchased wooden frames,
   finished or raw
paint (we used a pearlescent
   off-white paint to match the
   pearly buttons)
paintbrush
buttons
hot glue gun and glue sticks
mirror, cut to size at a glass
   supplier's

Method

1. If you are using a raw frame, give it a couple of coats of paint, allowing it to dry between the coats. A finished frame can be used as it is.

2. Arrange buttons around the frame until you are happy with the placement. Using a glue gun, glue each button in its place until the frame is covered. Wipe away any glue threads.

3. Place a mirror in the frame (if using), or a photograph.

> **TIP**
> Packets of colour-matched buttons are available at craft stores and larger fabric stores. Junk shops can also be a good place to pick up jars of old buttons. If you have a particular colour scheme in mind, start a collection of suitable buttons. Finding them is half the fun.

butterfly noticeboard

Who would have thought a noticeboard could be this glamorous? Fabric, ribbon and butterfly pins transform an everyday corkboard into something sensational.

Materials

cork noticeboard with wooden frame
paint, in two shades of blue
small paintbrush
fabric (to cover the cork)
ribbon (several metres will be required)
decorative tacks or nailheads
staple gun and staples
fabric glue
narrow quad beading
fine nails or glue to secure the beading
fabric butterflies
round-headed pins
hot glue gun and glue sticks
tape measure, pencil, scissors,
   adhesive tape

Method

1. Paint the noticeboard's wooden frame and leave to dry. Measure the inside dimensions of the frame and add 2cm to each dimension (height and width). Cut fabric to these dimensions and press a 1cm hem on all four edges. Use a staple gun to secure fabric to the corkboard, keeping staples as close to the fabric's edge as possible.

2. Lay out the ribbon in a grid over the noticeboard. Starting at the top left-hand corner, place one end of the ribbon 10cm in from the corner on the top edge. Secure its end to the frame with tape, then lay the ribbon flat across the board to the bottom right-hand corner, using tape to secure it 10cm up from the corner along the right edge of the frame. Cut the ribbon and repeat the process, laying a strip 10cm down from the top left corner along the left edge, to 10cm in from the bottom right corner along the bottom edge. Secure with adhesive tape and cut the ribbon.

3. Repeat this from top right to bottom left corners. Measure the distance between the two ribbons (it should be about 14–15cm) and use this measurement to place parallel pieces of ribbon across the board in both directions. Continue until the grid is complete.

4. Work the ribbons so they weave under and over alternately where they cross. Remove adhesive tape at one end of the ribbon to do this.

5. Staple ribbons to the board, keeping staples very close to the frame so that they will be hidden by the beading. Remove the adhesive tape; use sharp scissors to trim the ribbon ends close to the staples.

6. Lift the ribbons carefully where they cross over and place a dob of fabric glue underneath the bottom ribbon, then a dob between the two ribbons. Allow to dry.

7. Push decorative tacks or nailheads into the centre of the crosses. If the fabric and ribbon is thick and the nailheads do not push all the way through, add a dob of hot glue to help secure the nailheads.

8. Cut the beading to fit the inside measurements of the frame. Paint, then leave to dry. Glue beading in place at the inside edge of the frame, so it covers the staples and the edges of the ribbons.

9. Make the butterfly pins by pushing round-headed pins through the fabric butterflies. If the butterflies slip down the pins, a small dab of hot glue on the underside should secure them in place.

STAPLE THE RIBBONS
Staple the ends of the ribbon as close as you can to the edge of the noticeboard.

MAKE THE PINS
Push the pins through the fabric butterflies. Add a little dab of hot glue to their underside to hold them securely in place.

shadowboard for tools

Keep your garden tools in order by storing them on a blue-painted shadowboard. It's an adaptation of a toolshed favourite, with added style.

Materials

sheet of masonite peg board
paint, in two shades of blue (a sample pot should be enough, or you can use paint left over from other household jobs)
small paint roller and tray
large stencil brush or small paintbrush
very fine paintbrush (for touch-ups)
masking tape and heavy art paper or brown paper
repositionable spray adhesive
packet of assorted hooks
craft knife
garden tools

Method

1. Lay the peg board on the ground and lay out the garden tools on top of it. Place smaller tools at the top and larger tools at the bottom. When you are happy with the arrangement, record the position of the tools for reference; draw a quick sketch or take a photograph.
2. Use a small roller and paint tray to apply one or two coats of the background colour all over the board. Allow the paint to dry.
3. While the paint is drying, lay out a sheet of heavy art paper or brown paper the same size as the peg board. Referring to your sketch or photograph, lay out the garden tools in position and trace around their shapes. Spray the back of the paper with repositionable spray adhesive, then cut out the shapes using a craft knife.
4. Lay the paper out on the peg board; press it down so the adhesive keeps it in place. Secure around the outside with masking tape.
5. Using the other shade of paint and a large stencil brush or small paintbrush, paint over the cut-out holes, being careful that paint does not leak under the edges of the paper. You will need to do two coats, so do not remove the paper until the second coat is dry.
6. Carefully remove the paper and the masking tape. Use a fine paintbrush to touch up any accidental leakage (the holes in the board can allow paint to leak under the edges of the paper a little) or areas where the paint has been lifted by the adhesive.
7. When the paint is completely dry, add the hooks in the appropriate places and hang the garden tools over their shadows. We included a pair of hooks to hold a reel of twine, using a pencil passed through its centre as a spindle. The pencil may be used for writing on seedling markers or for making notes about any garden jobs that need to be done.

TRACING OUTLINES
Lay out the tools in position on the piece of paper. Remember to allow space for any straps on the handles that are used for hanging. Trace around the tools.

PAINTING THE SHAPES
Press the paper sheet onto the painted pegboard, so the spray adhesive keeps it in place. Carefully paint over the cut-out shapes in a second colour.

fabric-covered table

Putting on a fabric cover gives a softer look to a new table and is a clever way to revive an old one with a damaged top.

Materials

table
vinyl flock-backed upholstery padding
sturdy woven fabric (preferably upholstery
  fabric but heavy curtain fabric will do)
staple gun and staples
upholstery tacks (approximately 150–200
  for a medium-size table)
tack hammer and scrap of batting or soft,
  thick fabric and rubber band
tailor's chalk or pencil
measuring tape
sewing cotton
sharp scissors

MEASURING UP

To work out the dimensions for the table padding, allow the length of the table top, twice its thickness and 4cm (2cm at each end) for turn over. (If the legs are closer to the edges of the table top than 2cm you may need to adjust the turn-over measurement.) For the width, add together the width of the table top, twice its thickness and 4cm. Cut a piece of vinyl upholstery padding to these dimensions.

Method

1. Measure the dimensions of the table top (the one pictured measures 125 x 85cm), and its thickness (ours was 2cm).
2. Work out the dimensions for the upholstery padding (see box) and cut to size. Lay it flock-side up on the floor and lay the table top upside down in its centre. Using sharp scissors, cut away a square at the corners of the padding so when it's folded there is no overlap.
3. Fold up one short side of the padding over the table top and hold in place. Use sharp scissors to cut away a small triangle from the corner of the padding to form a mitre on the table's underside. Staple padding to the table's underside, putting in staples 5–10mm from the edge and parallel to the table's edge. Staple the other corners.
4. Staple the long sides of the padding, working from the centre, with staples 5–10mm in from the edge and no more then 10cm apart. Pull the padding tight as you go, but don't stretch it.
5. Take the dimensions for the upholstery padding and add another 2cm to both the length and the width. Cut fabric to this size. Press a 1cm hem under on all sides, and press any creases out of the fabric.
6. Lay fabric on floor wrong-side up and place the table top in its centre. The corners of the fabric will be folded, but cut a small triangle (about the width of the hem) off each corner to reduce bulk.
7. Holding fabric taut, staple it in the centre of each side, placing staples 5mm from the fabric's hemmed edge. Working around the table, staple fabric halfway between the centre staple and each corner.
8. At one corner, fold the shorter edge of the fabric over and place a staple in the hem, 2cm in from the long side of the table top. Use your fingers to crease the remainder of the fabric over the side of the table, so it sits neatly. Staple in place. Repeat at each corner.
9. Go around the table, adding staples so they are about 5cm apart.
10. Turn the table onto its side. Wrap padding around the head of the hammer and secure with a rubber band. Hammer tacks into the corners, placed so they're in the middle of the table's edge.
11. Slip a piece of sewing cotton behind the corner tack heads and stretch it along the edge of the table top as a guide to keep the tacks centred. Mark the positions for the remaining tacks with tailor's chalk or a pencil. They should be equally spaced, no more than 5cm apart.
12. Place a tack at each marked point and gently hammer it in. Do one side, then do the opposite side, then the ends.

To attach the padding, fold up one short side over the table top and hold it in place. Cut away a small triangle from the corner of the padding so that you can form a mitre on the table's underside. Staple the padding to the table's underside, putting in staples 5 to 10mm from the edge of the padding and parallel to the table's edge. Repeat the process on the other corners.

When you staple on the fabric, hold it taut, but don't stretch it out of shape. On the corners, fold the shorter edge of the fabric over and place a staple in the hem, around 2cm in from the long side of the table top. Use your fingers to crease the remainder of the fabric over the side of the table, causing a fold to form. Bring this fold up so that it sits neatly along the corner of the table. Fold the remaining fabric over the table edge and staple it in place. Repeat at each corner. Finish going around the table, adding staples so they are about 5cm apart. Place the staples parallel to the edge of the table.

To put in the tacks, wrap some thick batting or padding around the hammer's head and secure it with a rubber band. This prevents the hammer marking the tacks. Hammer the tacks into the corners first, placing them so they're in the middle of the table's edge. Work out roughly how far apart you wish the tacks to be spaced. The maximum spacing between tack centres should be no more than 5cm (about 4cm between the edges of the tack heads). Measure the distance between the two corner tacks on each side and choose a spacing that can be equally divided into this number. Mark the points for the remaining tacks with tailor's chalk or a pencil.

framed pinboard

This pinboard works best using a frame with an extravagant moulded pattern. Painting it in a flat white will tone it down and let your collectables be the star.

Materials

frame with patterned moulding
Canite to fit the frame (get it cut to
   size at the hardware store)
water-based sealer undercoat (we
   used Zinzar 123)
paint for top coat (we used a flat
   ceiling white for a chalky look)
Selleys Liquid Nails
pins or tacks
framer's tape or adhesive tape
pencil
2 small screw eyes and hanging
   wire or cord

Method

1. Accurately measure the area where a piece of glass fits in the frame. This is where the pinboard will go. Get the Canite cut to size.
2. Wipe the frame clean. Paint one coat of good quality water-based sealer undercoat and leave to dry. Paint two top coats and leave to dry. (The Canite comes already coloured white on one side.)
3. Turn the frame over. Squeeze out a thin line of Liquid Nails along the edges of the Canite and carefully slot it into the frame. Remove any excess with a clean rag. Use pins or tacks to keep the Canite in place until the adhesive dries. Remove the pins.
4. Use the framer's tape or adhesive tape to cover the join between the Canite and the frame.
5. Mark the position for the screw eyes one-third of the way down the frame. Screw them in, then attach wire or cord between them so you can hang the pinboard.

PAINTING THE FRAME
Paint the frame with one coat of water-based sealer and two top coats of white for a long-lasting finish.

INSERTING THE CANITE
Squeeze a thin line of Liquid Nails along the edges of the Canite and slot into the frame.

FINISHING THE BACK
After the Liquid Nails has dried, lay a piece of framer's tape or wide adhesive over the join between the frame and the Canite.

TIP
Wind a screw into the nozzle of the Liquid Nails after you use it. This will stop the adhesive in the end of the nozzle from hardening, keeping it ready for the next gluing job.

stencils on mirror

A flutter of butterflies adds a sweet touch to a simple mirror. Stencilling them on is remarkably easy, and you can update the design whenever you like.

Materials

mirror
stencil (we used the MS36 Butterfly stencil
    from Stencil Gallery)
3M Repositionable Spray Adhesive
masking tape and newspaper
large stencil brush
Folk Art enamel in white (this paint is
    suitable for glass and ceramics)
roll of paper towel

Method

1. Clean the mirror. Tape the stencil to some paper on the wall, then lightly spray the stencil's back with repositionable adhesive. You will get the best coverage by spraying the stencil while it's upright. Leave to dry for 20 seconds, so the glue is tacky.
2. Place the stencil in position on the mirror.
3. Lightly dip the brush in the paint. Then, using a circular motion, rub the bristles on a roll of paper towel to take off the excess paint. The brush should be quite dry.
4. Apply the paint through the stencil, using a light pouncing motion to create a stipple effect. Keep the brush vertical to do this.
5. Leave the paint to dry. As so little paint is used, it should dry almost immediately.
6. Remove the stencil from the mirror. The glue should still be tacky, so position the stencil to paint the next butterfly and repeat.

SPRAY ON THE ADHESIVE
Tape the stencil to some paper on a wall before you spray on the adhesive. You'll get better coverage if the stencil is in a vertical position.

PREPARE THE BRUSH
After dipping the brush in the paint, rub the bristles in a circular motion on a roll of paper towel. This removes excess paint; in fact, the bristles should be quite dry.

DABBING ON PAINT
Keep the brush vertical as you lightly pounce it onto the stencil. The idea is to create a cloud of white.

TIPS

• Wash the brush in cold water immediately after use, and leave to dry with the bristles upright.
• The paint used here gives a permanent finish. If you don't want a permanent pattern, use a paint such as Jo Sonja's artist acrylic in Titanium White. If you do this, remember that the design may come off if you wash the mirror.

175

CUT-OUT FLOWER CARD
(ACTUAL SIZE) PAGE 75

DAISY WHEELS CARD AND
ENVELOPE WITH DAISY
(ACTUAL SIZE) PAGE 66

SEQUINED SINGLET
(ACTUAL SIZE) PAGE 53

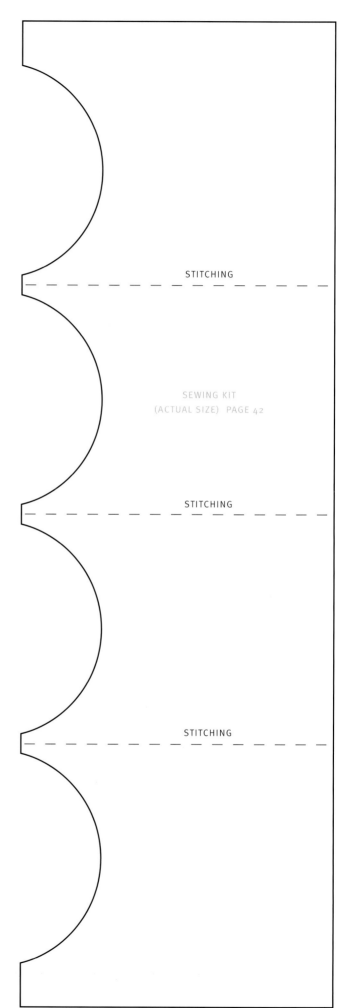

STITCHING

SEWING KIT
(ACTUAL SIZE) PAGE 42

STITCHING

STITCHING

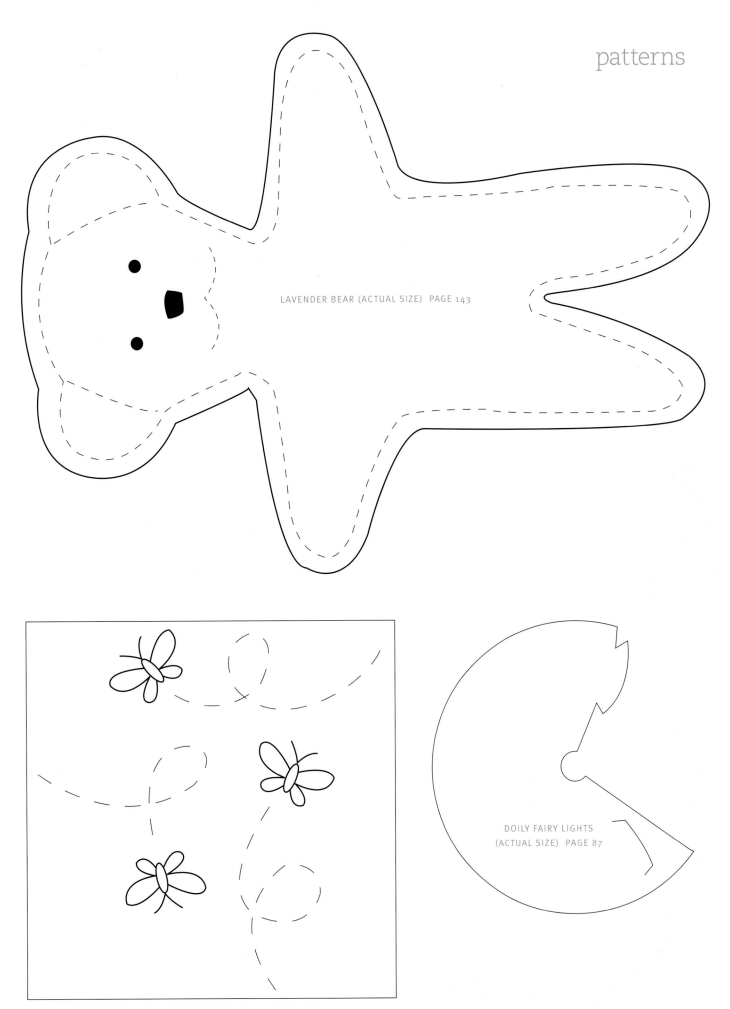

LAVENDER BEAR (ACTUAL SIZE) PAGE 143

DOILY FAIRY LIGHTS
(ACTUAL SIZE) PAGE 87

HERB SACHETS (ACTUAL SIZE) PAGE 140

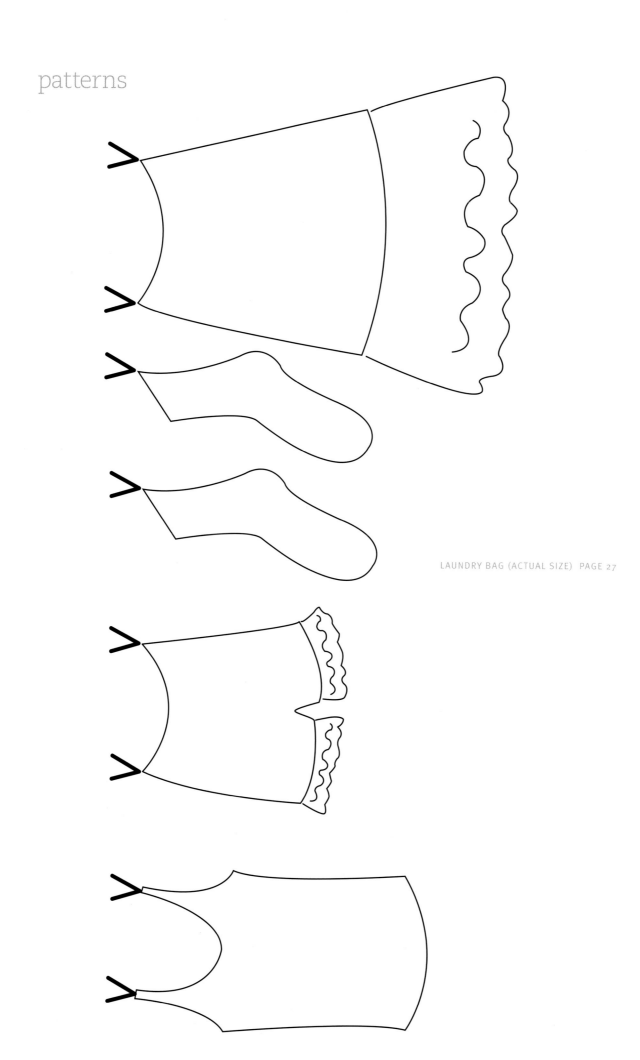

LAUNDRY BAG (ACTUAL SIZE) PAGE 27

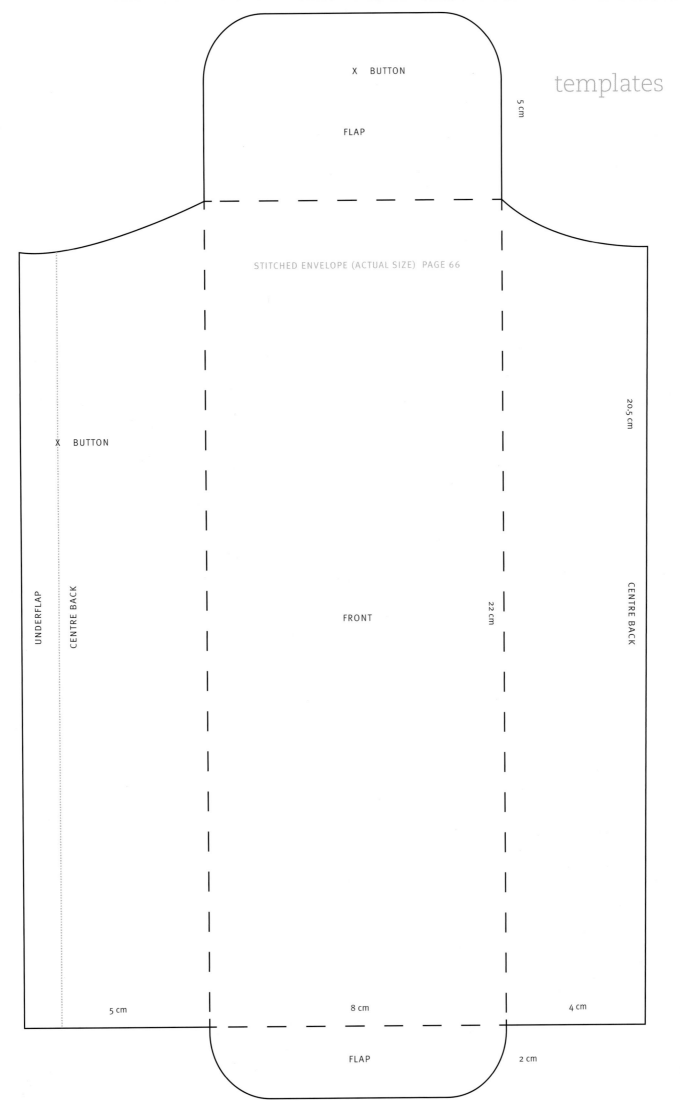

X   BUTTON

FLAP

5 cm

STITCHED ENVELOPE (ACTUAL SIZE) PAGE 66

20.5 cm

X   BUTTON

UNDERFLAP

CENTRE BACK

CENTRE BACK

FRONT

22 cm

5 cm

8 cm

4 cm

FLAP

2 cm

179

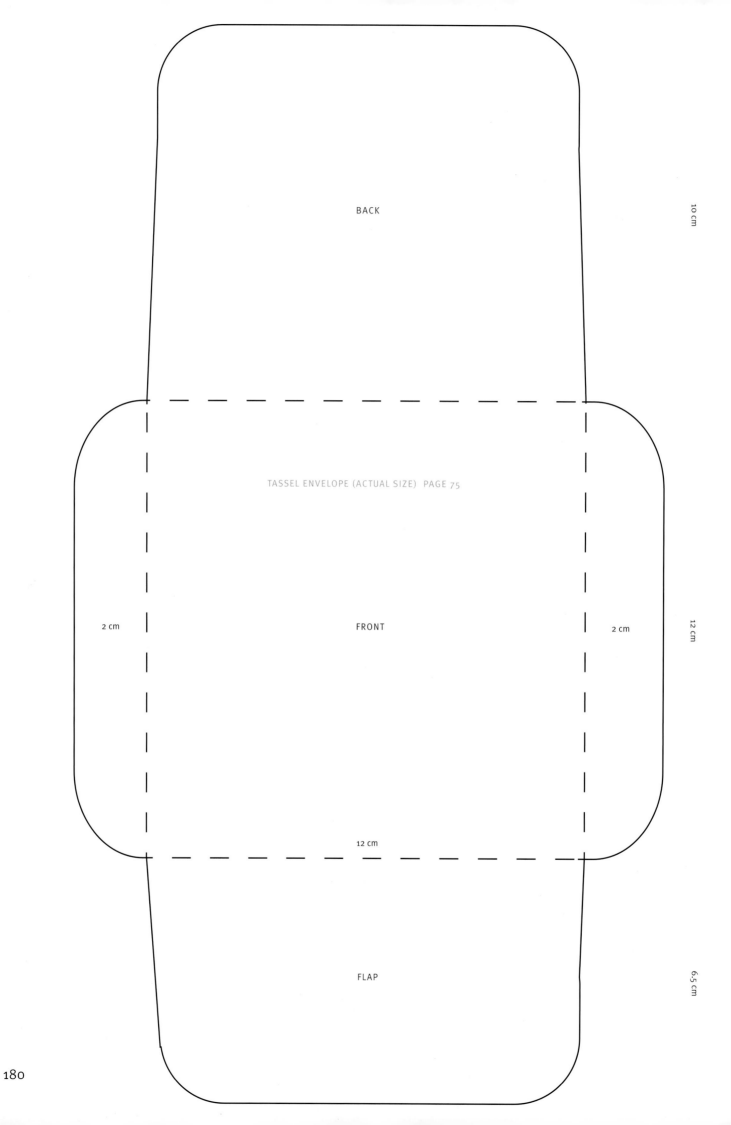

BACK

10 cm

TASSEL ENVELOPE (ACTUAL SIZE) PAGE 75

2 cm

FRONT

2 cm

12 cm

12 cm

FLAP

6.5 cm

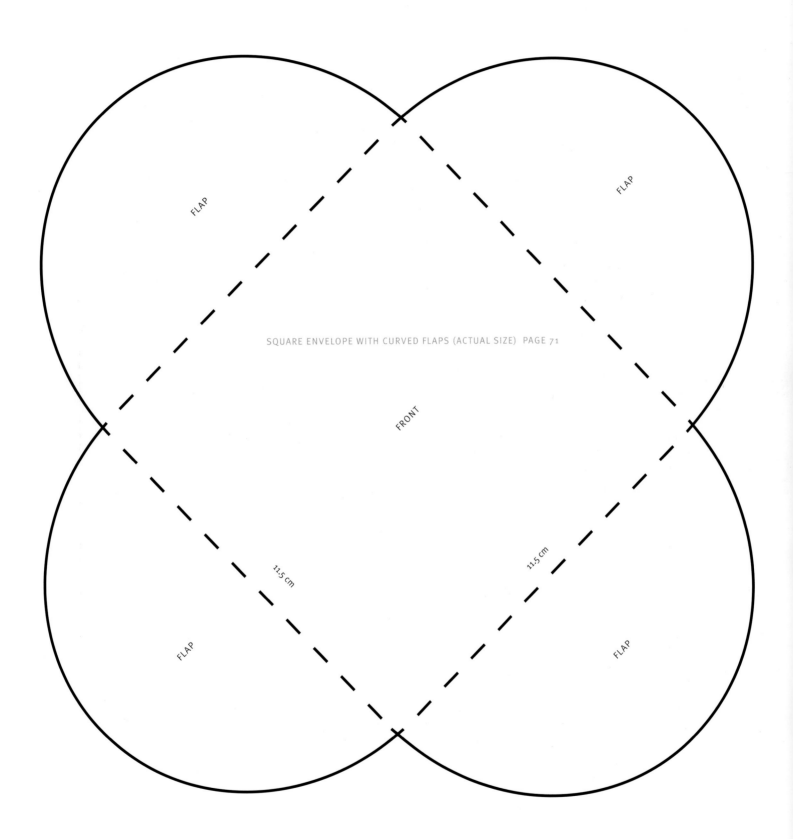

FLAP

FLAP

SQUARE ENVELOPE WITH CURVED FLAPS (ACTUAL SIZE) PAGE 71

FRONT

11.5 cm

11.5 cm

FLAP

FLAP

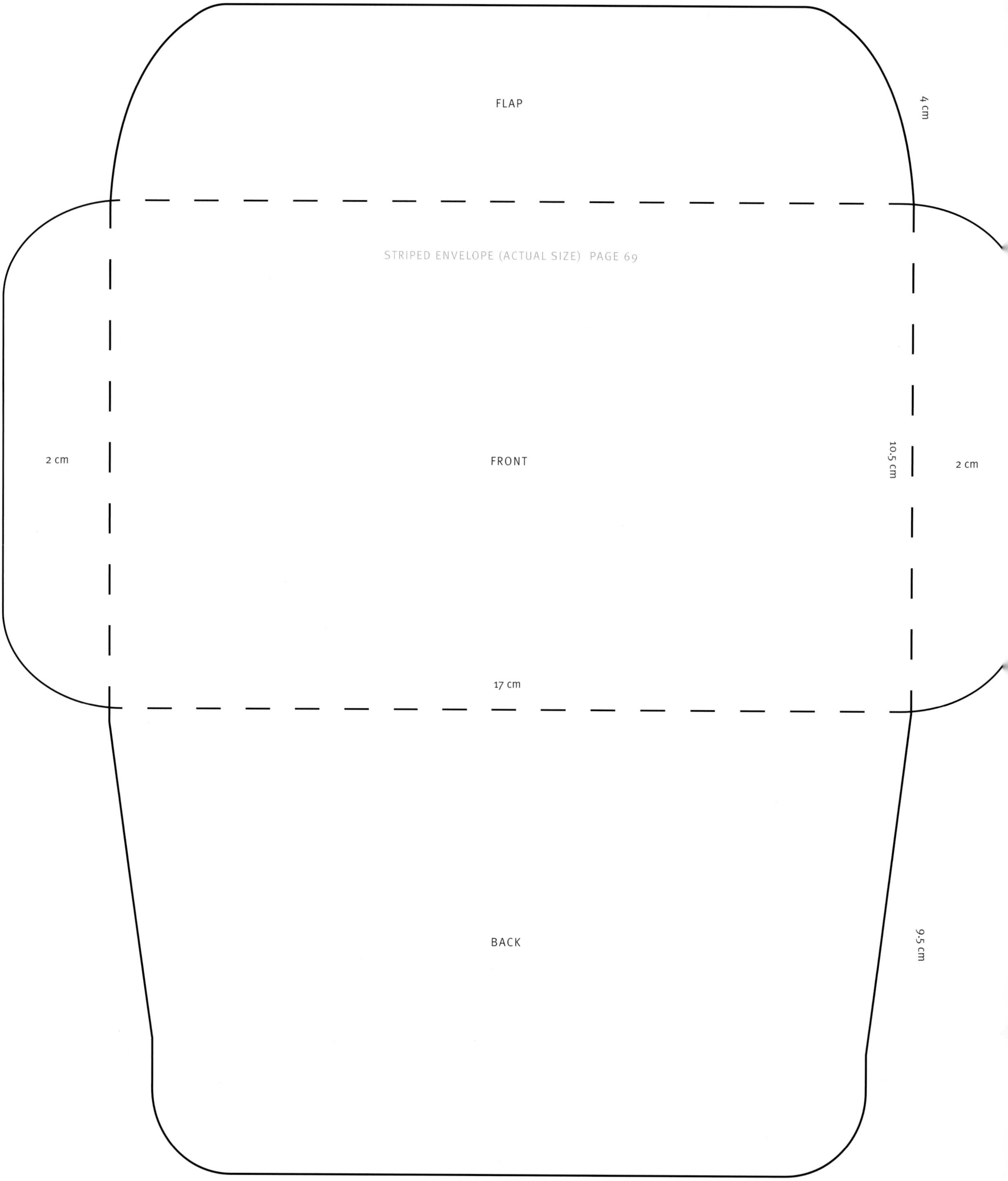

templates

FLAP

4 cm

STRIPED ENVELOPE (ACTUAL SIZE) PAGE 69

2 cm

10.5 cm

FRONT

2 cm

17 cm

BACK

9.5 cm

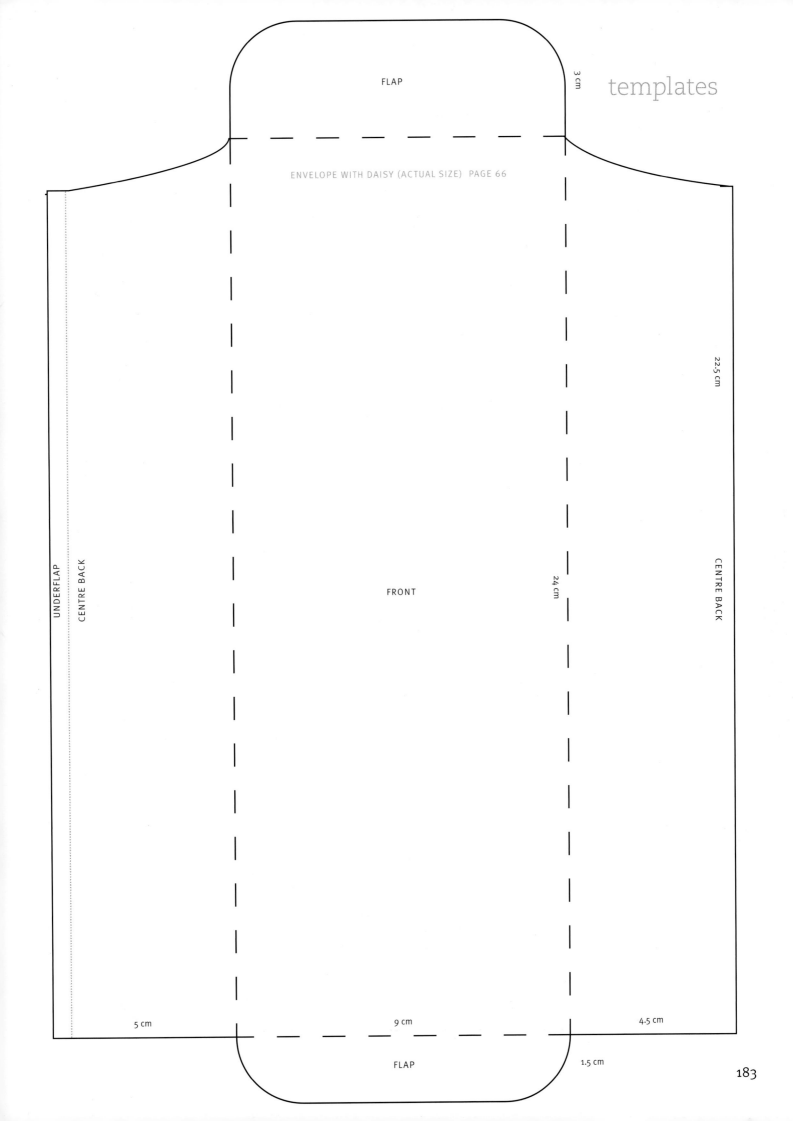

FLAP

3 cm

ENVELOPE WITH DAISY (ACTUAL SIZE) PAGE 66

22.5 cm

UNDERFLAP

CENTRE BACK

FRONT

24 cm

CENTRE BACK

5 cm

9 cm

4.5 cm

FLAP

1.5 cm

183

basic knitting

CASTING ON ONE-NEEDLE METHOD

Important: For the length of yarn in your left hand, allow 15cm for every 10 stitches, or three times the width of the article to be knitted. Slip loop onto needle (step 1) allowing sufficient length to cast on stitches. Hold this length in your left hand, passing it around your left thumb (step 2). Place point of needle beneath the loop on your thumb (step 3). Hold yarn from the ball in your right hand. Wrap yarn from ball around the point of the needle and draw through loop on the thumb (step 4). Draw up stitch on needle; pull both ends of yarn firmly (step 5). Repeat until required stitches are cast on.

CASTING ON TWO-NEEDLE METHOD

Make a slip loop 10cm from the end of the yarn and put onto the left-hand needle. Insert right-hand needle into loop and wind yarn from ball under and over the needle (step 1). Draw new loop through the first loop on the left-hand needle (step 2). Pass new loop onto the left-hand needle. Place point of right-hand needle between the two loops on the left-hand needle. Wind yarn under and over the right-hand needle point. Draw the new loop through between the two stitches on the left-hand needle. Slip the loop onto the left-hand needle (step 3). Repeat until required stitches are cast on.

CASTING OFF

To cast off on a knit row, knit the first two stitches, then with the point of the left-hand needle, lift the first stitch over the second stitch, leaving one stitch on the right-hand needle. Knit the next stitch, then again lift the first stitch over the second stitch, leaving one stitch on the right-hand needle. Continue in this way until one stitch remains on the needle. Cut the yarn, then pull it tight through the final stitch. If you are casting off on a purl row, purl rather than knit the stitches. If casting off ribbed work, lift each stitch over the next stitch following the pattern of the knitting.

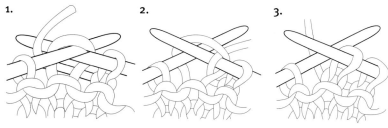

KNIT STITCH

Insert right-hand needle point through the first stitch on the left-hand needle from front to back (step 1). Wrap yarn clockwise around the point of the right-hand needle. Draw the new loop through and retain on the right-hand needle (step 2). Slip the first loop off the left-hand needle (step 3).

1.  **2.**  **3.**

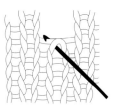

PURL STITCH

Hold the yarn at the front of the right-hand needle. Insert right-hand needle point through the first stitch on the left-hand needle from back to front. Keeping yarn in front of the needles, wrap anti-clockwise over the point of the right-hand needle (step 1). Draw the new loop through the stitch on the left-hand needle (step 2). Slip the first loop off the left-hand needle (step 3).

PICKING UP A DROPPED STITCH

Use a crochet hook to pick up a dropped stitch. Work on alternate sides for plain knitting (right side only for stocking stitch), and when the stitch is back in place slip it onto the knitting needle and continue work.

INCREASING

To increase, knit twice into the same stitch. First knit into the front of the stitch in the usual way, then before slipping the stitch off the left-hand needle, knit into the back loop of the stitch. When knitting into the back loop, bring the right-hand needle out behind the front loop. The same method is used on purl stitches.

DECREASING

To decrease, knit two stitches together. To do this, slip the right-hand needle point from left to right through two stitches instead of one, and then knit in the usual way. (To purl two stitches together, insert needle from right to left.)

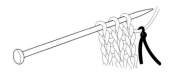

JOINING NEW YARN

Always join a new ball of yarn at the end of a row. Knot it on with a slip loop and darn in the ends when the piece is completed.

1. 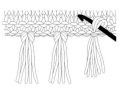 **2.** 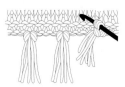 **3.**

MAKING A FRINGE

Take six 45cm strands of yarn and fold them in half. Use a crochet hook to draw the loop through the edge of the knitting (step 1).

Draw the ends of the yarn through the loop and pull tight (step 2).

Repeat evenly across the end of the garment (step 3).

basic embroidery

STARTING AND FINISHING

To start, thread the needle and make a knot in the end of the thread. Anchor the knot with a few stitches then continue working the embroidery. When you have finished stitching, you can snip off the initial knot so the thread lies flat yet secure.

To finish off, work one or two backstitches into the reverse side of the piece so they don't show on the front, then snip thread.

RUNNING STITCH

Working from right to left, pass the needle over and under the fabric, either keeping the stitches even, or having the under stitches half as long as the upper ones. Take several stitches on the needle before drawing it through.

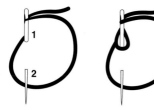

CHAIN STITCH

Pull thread through to the right side of the fabric. Hold the thread with your thumb to make a loop, then do a stitch as shown, starting at the same hole where the thread came up. Do not pull thread too tightly, as you want to keep the loops. To finish a row of chain stitch, take a small stitch over the last chain loop.

BACKSTITCH

Bring the needle through to the right side of the fabric and make a small stitch backwards, then bring the needle through a little in front of the first stitch. Work from right to left.

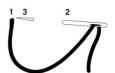

STEM STITCH

This is like backstitch, but it's worked from left to right. Make a sloping stitch along the line of the design, then bring the needle out halfway along this first stitch.

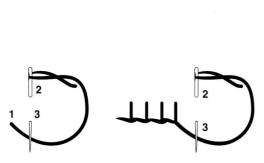

BLANKET STITCH

A finishing stitch for edges, blanket stitch is worked from left to right. Pull the needle through to the front of the fabric, near to its edge. Do another stitch to the right as shown, and hold the thread under the point of the needle as you pull it through.

method 1.　　**method 2.**

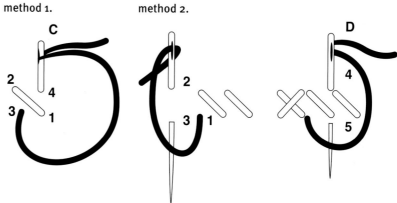

CROSS STITCH

Cross stitch may be worked as individual stitches or in a long row. The crosses may be marked on the fabric, worked on a material with a uniform weave, or on checked gingham. Make a slanting stitch from the lower right to the upper left corner of cross, then another from the lower left to the upper right corner (method 1). Work all the crosses the same way to give a uniform appearance. If you're working long rows with the same colour, do one row of stitches slanting in one direction, then work back and cross all stitches in the other direction (method 2).

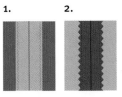

basic sewing

SEWING ON A BUTTON

Hold the button in place, and push the needle from the back of the fabric up through one of the holes. Stitch until the thread has gone through the holes five or six times. Pull needle and thread through to between the button and the fabric, and wrap the thread several times around the exposed threads under the button to make a shank. Tie off the thread under the button.

BASTING OR TACKING

This is a line of running stitch (see Basic Embroidery) which holds fabric pieces together before they are machine stitched. The basting is unpicked after the machine stitching is completed. It's a good idea for novices to baste seams before machine stitching, as it holds the fabric firmly in place and makes for easier sewing.

SEWING A SEAM

Put right sides of fabric together and pin where the seam will be. The usual seam allowance (the distance from the edge of the fabric to the line of stitching) is 1.5cm. If you put in the pins crossways to the fabric's edge, they can be stitched over. Do a few reverse-stitches at the beginning of the seam to keep it from unravelling, then stitch forward to make the seam. When you reach the end, reverse-stitch again for 1cm. Press the seam open.

NEATENING A SEAM

Neatening, or finishing, a seam's raw edges stops the fabric from unravelling. You can either stitch a row of zigzag close to the edges, then trim close to the stitching (diagram 1); or do a line of straight-stitch about 5mm in from the edges, then trim with pinking shears (diagram 2).

basic crochet

SLIP KNOT

To start your crochet, make a loop, insert the crochet hook through its centre, then pull the long end of the yarn downward to tighten the loop.

CHAIN STITCH

With the hook held in your right hand and the yarn held taut with the fingers of your left hand, lower the crochet hook under then over the yarn to grab a loop. Pull this loop through the slip knot already on the hook.

SLIP STITCH

This is used mainly for joining. Insert the hook through the stitch of a previous round. Draw a loop through the stitch and the loop on the hook in one movement.

DOUBLE CROCHET

Insert hook through two loops of chain stitch on previous round, then draw a loop through, then draw another loop through both loops on the hook. (If not a chain stitch on the previous round, then insert hook through two threads of the stitch on the previous row.)

TREBLE

Loop yarn over hook, then insert hook into next chain, then draw a loop through, then draw another loop through the first two loops on the hook, then draw another loop through the remaining two loops on the hook.

DOUBLE TREBLE

Loop yarn twice over hook, insert hook into next chain and draw a loop through, then draw another loop through the first two loops on the hook, then draw another loop through the next two loops on the hook, then draw another loop through the remaining two loops on the hook.

JOINING NEW YARN

Change colours at the beginning of a round. Snip the yarn, leaving a few centimetres. Finish with a slip stitch and pull tight. To bring in new yarn, insert hook for first stitch, hook new yarn, and then pull it through, leaving it looped on the hook. Catch both ends of yarn and pull through. Let the loose end of yarn lie so it is covered by the stitches as you work. Any loose ends may be darned in when the piece is finished.

techniques

basic beading

THREADING A BEADING NEEDLE

Beading needles have a very small eye so they can pass through the centre of beads. The easiest way to thread one is to first make a small 'leader loop' with a very fine coloured thread. To do this, thread about 6cm of fine silk thread or one filament from a strand of stranded embroidery cotton through the needle's eye and tie with a knot to make a loop. Draw the beading thread through the loop to begin work.

OVERHAND KNOT

This is the simplest and most widely used knot. You make an overhand loop, then pull the end of the thread through the loop.

HALF-HITCH KNOT

This is a neat way to secure the ends a thread. Pass the end of the thread over and around the standing part, then pull it through the resulting loop.

basic DIY

PAINTING

Choose a suitably sized brush for the job in hand. For the projects in this book, a small 50mm paintbrush or a smaller fitch brush are appropriate. Never overload the brush with paint. Pour the paint into an empty can, no more than one-third full, then dip no more than one-third of the brush's bristles into the paint. Gently tap each side of the brush on the inside of the can three or four times, then wipe the bristles on the inside lip of the can. (Alternatively, you can stretch a piece of wire across the paint can and wipe the bristles on that.) Spread the paint evenly on the surface. If you have used water-based paint, clean brushes by washing them in warm soapy water, then in clean water. Roll the brush handle between your hands to spin off excess water, then place it handle-end down in a container to dry. Once dry, wrap the bristles in plastic film. For oil-based paint, clean brushes with turps, then wash them as above.

HAMMERING IN NAILS

An ordinary claw hammer is suitable for most nailing jobs. Hold the nail between your thumb and forefinger and tap it in gently with the hammer until it stands on its own. Strike the head squarely with the hammer until the nail is driven all the way in. To remove a nail, place a small scrap of wood as a cushion under the hammer's head, and use the claw end as a lever.

SCREWING IN SCREWS

Make a pilot hole in the spot where you want the screw to go. For smaller screws (size 5 and smaller), place the end of a nail on the screwhole and tap in place with a hammer, or make a hole with an awl. For larger screws, drill a hole with an appropriately sized drill bit. (For screw sizes 5, 6 and 7, use a 1.5mm bit; for screw sizes 8 and 9, a 2.0mm bit; for size 10, a 2.4mm bit; and for 12 and 14, a 2.8mm bit). Choose a screwdriver with a blade that fills the screw's slot, both in width and thickness. Use a Phillips head screwdriver on screws with a cross-slotted head. Place the point of the screw in the pilot hole and screw in place. Make sure you keep the screwdriver and screw straight.

USING A STAPLE GUN

To use a staple gun, grasp the hand-hold and position the gun firmly on the material to be stapled. Release the safety lock, release your grip, and then squeeze the handle sharply to fire the staple. Press on the head of the staple gun with the heel of your free hand while you staple. Staple guns must be kept out of reach of children and have the safety handle locked when not in use.

SAWING

Panel saws (all-purpose saws) and ripsaws (which cut along the grain of the wood) are used in a similar way. Firmly secure the item to be cut. Hold the handle with your index finger pointing down to the end of the blade. Place your thumb on one side of the cutting line to help guide the saw. Start by pulling the blade towards you once or twice to make a small groove. Take your thumb away, then start pushing the saw through the wood at a 45-degree angle if you're using a panel saw, or at a steeper 60-degree angle for a ripsaw. Use all the blade and push down from your shoulder, not your elbow. Don't apply any force when pulling the saw back. Support the end of the waste wood as you near the end of the cut. A hacksaw is used with a hand on each end and you cut straight across, rather than downwards.

Page 6 Hammer, brushes, mohair and knitting needles from Spotlight; 1300 305 405, www.spotlight.com.au. Pitcher by Typhoon; 1800 651 146. Butterfly from Lincraft; 1800 640 107, www.lincraft.com.au. Pencil cup, coloured pencils and A5 journal from kikki.K; (03) 9645 6346, www.kikki-k.com.au. Photo journal from Paper Couture, Paddington, NSW; (02) 9357 6855.

Page 13 Cotton slip by Lee Mathews; (02) 9997 3787, www.leemathews.com.au.

Page 14 Drawstring pants by Lee Mathews, as before. Sheets by Aura; (03) 9552 6090, www.auralifestyle.com.

Page 17 Oxford pillowcase and Country Club coverlet by Peri Homeworks; (02) 9565 4960, www.peri.com.au.

Page 18-21 Stencil supplied by Stencil Gallery; (02) 9518 7895, www.stencil gallery.com.au. Sheets by Aura, as before. Aspen blanket by Peri Homeworks, as before.

Page 22 Sixten chair by IKEA; www.ikea.com.au.

Page 25 Cotton slip by Lee Mathews, as before.

Page 29 Cotton slip by Lee Mathews, as before.

Pages 32-35 Red fabric for picnic set from Bute Fabrics; www.butefabrics.co.uk. Australian distributor James Richardson; (02) 9310 7155, www.jamesrichardson.com.au.

Page 39 Seed crockery by Villa Homewares; 1800 443 366, www.villahomewares.com.au. Cutlery by Alex Liddy; 1300 763 833, www.housewares. com.au.

Page 40 White china by Alex Liddy, as before.

Page 43 Knitted throw rug by Peri Homeworks; (02) 9565 4960, www.peri.com.au.

Page 44 Mohair throw rug by Waverley Australia; (03) 6339 1106, www.waverleyaustralia. com.au. Urban chair by IKEA; www.ikea.com.au. White tumbler from Domayne; (02) 8339 7000, www. domayne.com.au.

Page 48 Cotton long-sleeve T-shirt by adam + eve; (02) 9319 4488, www.adampluseve.com.

Page 51 Sharp A-Line handbag by Catherine Manuell Design; (03) 9482 4877, www.catherine manuelldesign.com.au.

Page 56 Moroccan tea glasses and glass teapot from T2; (03) 9417 3722, www.T2tea.com.au.

Page 59 China and cutlery by Alex Liddy; 1300 763 833, www.housewares.com.au.

Page 67 Kitchen pitcher by Typhoon; 1800 651 146.

Page 70 Pitcher and oven mitt by Typhoon, as before. Ribbon from kikki.K; (03) 9645 6346, www.kikki-k.com.au.

Page 81 Shells from My Island Home; (02) 9362 8760, www.myislandhome.com.au.

Pages 98-99 Preserving jars from The Bay Tree, Woollahra, NSW; (02) 9328 1101, www.thebaytree.com.au. Tea-towel by Rhubarb; (03) 9429 9600, www.rhubarb. net.au. Colander from Domayne; (02) 8339 7000, www.domayne.com.au.

Page 101 Platter by Universal Enterprises; (03) 9415 8111, www.universal-ent.com.

Page 102 Covered boxes from Paper Couture, Paddington, NSW; (02) 9357 6855.

Page 105 Floral ribbon and takeaway boxes from Spotlight; 1300 305 405, www.spotlight.com.au.

Pages 106-107 Café platter and canister in caramel from Domayne; (02) 8339 7000, www.domayne.com.au. Paper napkins from Bayswiss; (02) 8595 6111, www. bayswiss.com.au.

Page 109 Reno canister and pink latte cup from Domayne, as before. Gift tag from Paper Couture, as before. Napkin from Bayswiss, as before.

Pages 110-111 Cooling rack and wooden spoon from Spotlight; 1300 305 405; www.spotlight.com.au. Pink tea-towel and bowl from Domayne; (02) 8339 7000, www.domayne.com.au.

Pages 112-113 Chef bowl from Domayne, as before. White serving dish, taupe pot mitt and tea-towel set from Spotlight, as before. Bamboo table runner from Bayswiss; (02) 8595 6111, www. bayswiss.com.au.

Page 114 Gingham ribbon from Spotlight, as before.

Pages 116-117 Pink stripe napkins from Bayswiss, as before. Ribbons from The Bay Tree, Woollahra, NSW; (02) 9328 1101, www.thebaytree.com.au. Gift tag from Paper Couture, Paddington, NSW; (02) 9357 6855. Door mat from Kmart; www.kmart.com.au.

Page 120 Blue colander and wooden pepper mill from Spotlight; 1300 305 405, www.spotlight.com.au. Glass bottles for oil and vinegar from Vicino; (02) 9698 7166. Apron by Thistledown; 0412 487 908, klochrin@optusnet.com.au. Flour-sack tea-towels from David Jones; 13 33 57, www.davidjones.com.au.

Page 122 Gift box from Opus, Paddington, NSW; (02) 9360 4803. Glass jars from IKEA; www.ikea.com.au. Fabrics, sewing notions, wool and knitting needles from Spotlight; 1300 305 405, www.spotlight.com.au.

Page 124 Wooden bin (used as a toy-box) from Myer; 1800 811 611, www.myer.com.au. Face washers, nappies and muslin wraps from Spotlight; 1300 305 405, www. spotlight.com.au. Bonds baby singlets; 1800 054 321, www. bonds.com.au. Baby Love by Robin Barker, Macmillan; www.panmacmillan.com.au. Baby Workshop by Aromababy Pure Baby Moisture Lotion and Great Expectation Relaxing Massage Oil; (03) 9464 0888, www.aromababy.com. L'Occitane en Provence Mom & Baby Balm; (02) 8912 3000, www.loccitane.com.au. Moët & Chandon champagne; www.moet.com.

Page 126 Glazed pot, garden fork and trowel from Sunrise Nursery, Helensburgh, NSW; (02) 4294 1307. Garden gloves by Hable Construction; www.hableconstruction.com. The Garden Book by Tim Richardson, Phaidon; www. phaidon.com. Watering can from The Reject Shop; (03) 9371 5555, www.rejectshop. com.au. Hemp Hand Protector cream from The Body Shop; 1800 065 232, www.the bodyshop.com.au.

Page 128 Galvanised tub and bath towels from IKEA; www. ikea.com.au. Australian House & Garden Sanctuary, ACP Books; (02) 9282 8618, www. acpbooks.com.au. T2 lemongrass tea; (03) 9417 3722, www.T2tea.com.au. L'Occitane en Provence Foaming Bath; (02) 8912 3000, www. loccitane.com.au. Jurlique Pure Rosewater Freshener; 1800 805 286, www.jurlique. com.au. Oil burner and oil from The Body Shop, as before. Peaceful Moments CD by Tony Vandermeer, distributed by MRA Entertainment; www. mraentertainment.com.

Pages 130-31 Twine from Paper Couture, Paddington, NSW; (02) 9357 6855. Burgon & Ball pocket pruner from Quality Products Direct; (02) 9999 0684, www.quality products.com.au. Flowers from Jute, Bondi Junction, NSW; (02) 9369 5559.

Page 134 Tea-light holder from Bayswiss; (02) 8595 6111, www.bayswiss.com.au.

Page 136 French market basket from The Market Basket Co.; (02) 9332 2031, www. themarketbasketco.com.au. Hydrangea wreath by The Floral Decorator, Erskineville, NSW; (02) 9516 3113. Stripe ribbon from The Bay Tree, Woollahra, NSW; (02) 9328 1101, www.thebaytree.com.au. Watering can from Bunnings; (03) 8831 9777, www. bunnings.com.au.

Page 137 Burgon & Ball pocket pruner from Quality Products Direct; (02) 9999 0684, www.qualityproducts.com.au.

Page 145 Bird decoration from Spotlight; 1300 305 405, www.spotlight.com.au.

Page 146-149 Perspex frames from IKEA; www.ikea.com.au. Pencil cup and pencils from kikki.K; (03) 9645 6346, www.kikki-k.com.au. Scissors from Spotlight, as before.

Page 154 Flowers from Pearsons Florist; (02) 9550 7777, www.pearsonsflorist.com.au.

Pages 156-157 Upholstery padding from Swadling's Timber Mitre 10, Rosebery, NSW; (02) 9317 2299. Nails, hammer and screwdriver from Kmart; www.kmart.com.au.

Page 160 Frames by Corban and Blair; (02) 9560 0122, www.corbanblair.com.au.

Page 164 Ribbon and fabric from no chintz; (02) 9958 0257, www.nochintz.com. Butterflies from Lincraft; 1800 640 107, www.lincraft.com.au. Marrakech votive from Papaya; (02) 9517 3055, www.papaya. com.au. Lantern Paper pocket journal from Paper Couture, Paddington, NSW; (02) 9357 6855. Pencils from Corban and Blair, as before.

Page 167 All garden tools from Quality Products Direct; (02) 9999 0684, www.quality products.com.au.

Pages 168-171 Björkudden table by IKEA; www.ikea. com.au. Cup and saucer, Shell vase and Marrakech votive from Papaya, as before. Pencil and Kraft journal, Corban and Blair; (02) 9560 0122, www. corbanblair.com.au. Lantern Paper pocket journal from Paper Couture, as before.

Page 173 Paper butterflies and journals (shown lying flat) from Paper Couture, Paddington, NSW; (02) 9357 6855. Leather jewel box, blue leather envelope, notebooks and storage boxes, all from kikki.K; (03) 9645 6346, www.kikki-k.com.au.

Page 174 Kolja mirror from IKEA; www.ikea.com.au. Stencil from Stencil Gallery; (02) 9518 7895, www.stencil gallery.com.au.

Special thanks to Summers Floral, Woollahra, NSW; (02) 9328 2475, www.summers floral.com, for our flowers.

index

AUSTRALIAN HOUSE & GARDEN MAGAZINE
Editorial director Anny Friis
Editor Maya Kelett
Style editor Fiona Duff

ACP BOOKS
Editorial director Susan Tomnay
Creative director Hieu Chi Nguyen
Creative consultant Louise Bickle
Project manager Jo McKinnon
Designer Lisa Cainero
Illustrations Jarrod Edwards, except for pg 142,
illustration by Louise Pfanner
Copy editing Megan Fisher, Christine Eslick
Pre-press Harry Palmer
Editorial co-ordinators Inga Kossowska,
Jaime Lee, Lisa Pin

Photography Andre Martin
Styling Louise Bickle, Jenni Booth
Additional photography Maree Homer (lavender
    bouquet on pg 134; hydrangeas on pg 136)
Food preparation Rebecca Squadrito
All recipes copyright ACP Books

Thanks to our project makers
Georgina Bitcon, Melody Lord,
Margaret Stork, Margaret Cox,
Meredith Kirton, Jo McComiskey,
Pearsons Florist, Stephen Prodes,
Dawn Stan, Bonnie Thompson,
Bryce Tibby, Lorna Williams,
Mark Williams, Jacqui Winn

Sales director Brian Cearnes
Marketing manager Bridget Cody
Production manager Cedric Taylor

Chief executive officer Ian Law
Group publisher Pat Ingram
General manager Christine Whiston

Produced by ACP Books, published by ACP Magazines Ltd.
54 Park St, Sydney NSW Australia 2000. GPO Box 4088, Sydney, NSW 2001.
Phone +61 2 9282 8618 Fax +61 2 9267 9438
acpbooks@acpmagazines.com.au www.acpbooks.com.au
To order books, phone 136 116.
Printed by SNP Leefung, China

Rights enquiries Laura Bamford, Director ACP Books. lbamford@acpmedia.co.uk

Australia Distributed by Network Services, GPO Box 4088, Sydney, NSW 2001.
Phone +61 2 9282 8777 Fax +61 2 9264 3278
networkweb@networkservicescompany.com.au
United Kingdom Distributed by Australian Consolidated Press (UK), Moulton Park
Business Centre, Red House Rd, Moulton Park, Northampton, NN3 6AQ.
Phone +44 1604 497 531 Fax +44 1604 497 533 books@acpmedia.co.uk www.acpuk.com
Canada Distributed by Whitecap Books Ltd, 351 Lynn Ave, North Vancouver, BC, V7J 2C4.
Phone +1 604 980 9852 Fax +1 604 980 8197 customerservice@whitecap.ca
www.whitecap.ca
New Zealand Distributed by Southern Publishers Group, 44 New North Road,
Eden Terrace, Auckland.
Phone +64 9 309 6930 Fax +64 9 309 6170 hub@spg.co.nz
South Africa Distributed by PSD Promotions, 30 Diesel Road Isando, Gauteng
Johannesburg.
PO Box 1175, Isando 1600, Gauteng Johannesburg.
Phone +27 11 392 6065/6/7 Fax +27 11 392 6079/80 orders@psdprom.co.za

Cataloguing-in-publication data:
Hand crafted: beautiful things to create at home.
Includes index.
ISBN-13 978-1-86396-513-2.
ISBN-10 1 86396 513 0.
1. Handicraft – Australia – Handbooks, manuals, etc.
I. Title: Australian House & Garden
745.5